WORD AND SPIRIT TOGETHER

WORD AND SPIRIT TOGETHER

Uniting Charismatics and Evangelicals

David Pawson

ANCHOR RECORDINGS

This edition published in Great Britain in 2014 by
Anchor Recordings Ltd
72, The Street, Kennington, Ashford TN24 9HS

For more of David Pawson's teaching,
including DVDs and CDs, go to
www.davidpawson.com

FOR FREE DOWNLOADS: www.davidpawson.org

For further information, email: info@davidpawsonministry.com

ISBN 978-1-909886-60-5

Printed by Lightning Source

Contents

Part I   THE DIFFERENCES REVIEWED

Part II   THE DIFFERENCES RESOLVED

PREFACE TO SECOND EDITION

When I wrote this book, the gap between 'charismatic' and 'evangelical' seemed to be closing. The distinction between the two labels was increasingly blurred. It looked as if one final effort would achieve integration.

Spring Harvest had done much to bring this about. Songs inspired by the charismatic renewal had penetrated most evangelical worship. Both streams were uniting to 'March for Jesus', though the agenda varied from witness to warfare.

So the whole situation has moved on. If 'a week in politics is a long time', then five years in Christian circles can be at least as significant, especially when change is fashionable. One has to run to catch up these days, even in the church, traditionally the most traditional part of society.

Some might therefore conclude that this book is already out of date, dealing with issues long since left behind. There is some truth in this but the question remains whether they ought to be left behind or simply shelved, either consciously or unconsciously, to be faced again later.

In some ways, Word and Spirit have been drifting apart again.

A healthy recovery of worship as an end in itself, as distinct from 'the preliminaries', has often affected both the priority and proportion in the service formerly given to systematic teaching, much of which is now topical rather than exegetical. The recent practice of climaxing corporate worship with individual 'ministry' has added further pressure. The Word is squeezed from both sides – worship before and ministry after (I have been asked quite frequently if I will 'minister' *after* I have spoken, to which I usually reply that I will be ministering *while* I speak!). The first and last parts of the meeting are often thought to be more stimulating, perhaps because they are more participatory but possibly because there is more happening visibly. In extreme cases, preaching and teaching take a back seat – unless the seats have been stacked away already, the carpet providing the basic physical needs of the congregation! A recent article in a national Christian magazine predicted that the 'sermon' would disappear from twenty-first century worship.

Contemporary culture emphasises experience, which means focusing on present encounters rather than future prospects. It is hardly surprising that this search for meaningful sensations, which in the world ranges from hallucinogenic drugs to exotic holidays, should appear among those coming into the church, especially in the younger generations.

Nor is it to be dismissed. We *need* to encounter God in reality. We need to *know* we have met him. Theology without experience is barren. But experience without theology is dangerous.

This is precisely where Word and Spirit need each other. It is through the Spirit that Word becomes part of our experience. The Bible is not just a record of what God has said and done in history; it is also an account of how these things were experienced by men and women like ourselves. And we can share that experience as the Spirit who inspired the Word invades and indwells our lives.

However, to seek experience in the Spirit without knowledge of the Word can be hazardous. Real religious sensations can come from at least three sources: divine, human and demonic. Lack of discernment and therefore discrimination can lead to confusion and even division among God's people. Scripture is the yardstick by which we may judge what is of the Spirit. At the height of excitement about what was happening at Toronto and elsewhere, I wrote a book called *Is the Blessing Biblical?* (now out of print), which pleased neither those who thought everything associated with that 'Move' was wonderful nor those who thought that it was all terrible! But it did seem to cool down some of the heat on both sides of the fence and open up dialogue again.

Incidentally, it was because the 'mixed blessing' of Toronto began to be labelled 'Fourth Wave' that I felt it wise to change the title of this book.

So far, I have been surveying some developments in the charismatic stream. Significantly, it is within this orbit that a new label has been coined: 'post-evangelical'. The Spirit is said to be moving us beyond scripture or at least away from the evangelical view of its inspiration and authority. It becomes difficult to see what criteria can then be used to judge genuine or false claims to be led by the Spirit, other than subjective intuition. Charismatics without evangelicals become vulnerable to being 'blown here and there by every eddy of teaching' (Eph. 4:14).

Evangelicals without charismatics are of equal concern. Sound doctrine does not ensure spiritual dynamic. Exegesis is no substitute for experience. The church is meant to be powerful as well as pure.

There has been a definite drift from the two distinctions of charismatics (see pages 33–34) in evangelical circles, in one case deliberate and the other by default.

The major factor has been the widespread rejection of the experience known as 'baptism in the Spirit'. This was the fundamental rediscovery of the pentecostal movement in the first half of the twentieth century, which was largely outside the older churches and was later called the 'first wave'. The 'second wave', during the next quarter century, introduced this experience and the gifts it released to the mainline denominations, both Catholic and Protestant.

The 'third wave', associated with the names of the late John Wimber and his colleague Peter Wagner, who coined the 'wave' labels, made a radical shift of emphasis. Perceiving that Spirit-baptism was the main stumbling-block for evangelicals, this was quietly dropped and the focus was on the exercise of 'spiritual gifts'. From then on the 'renewal' would be described as 'charismatic' (from the Greek word *charismata*, used for the gifts) rather than 'pentecostal' (which drew attention to the Spirit-baptisms in Acts, beginning in chapter 2).

This reduced 'charismatic' agenda achieved some success and many evangelicals ceased to be 'cessationist' (the belief that the more sensational gifts *ceased* when the original apostles passed away or when the New Testament was completed) and became 'open' to supernatural manifestations in church life today.

However, there was a price to pay for what in hindsight appears to be a compromise.

On the one hand, there was a noticeable decline in the exercise of spiritual gifts, after the initial euphoric welcome. Even unsympathetic observers have noted that these only appear with frequency and constancy where baptism in the Spirit is clearly and confidently preached and received.

On the other hand, the loss of this dimension left a vacuum in spiritual experience. Little wonder that this led to interest in alternative 'encounters' with God, often less biblical and even quite bizarre.

I was so alarmed by this serious loss of what I regarded as vital to the charismatic contribution, that I wrote *Jesus Baptises in One Holy Spirit* (1997, reprinted by Terra Nova Publications, 2006), which covers the biblical, theological, historical and pastoral aspects. My primary purpose was to restore interest in this crucial aspect of Jesus' messianic ministry, highlighted by John the Baptist in all four Gospels. But there was also an underlying aim of undergirding the concept with a fresh understanding of biblical theology.

Spirit baptism had not been omitted for diplomatic reasons alone. There was a genuine reservation among evangelical scholars about the 'pentecostal' teaching that was used to validate it. In particular, it had been regarded as a 'second blessing', subsequent to rather than part of initiation, and speaking in tongues was demanded as the only, and sufficient, evidence. Both emphases were widely rejected by evangelicals but, as yet, there has been no widely accepted alternative concept that includes the rediscovered insights. By default, both streams are reverting to the traditional evangelical position, which holds that Spirit baptism is synonymous and simultaneous with 'conversion' (sacramentalists would say 'with baptism') and is not inherently experiential, but frequently unconscious.

Many would rejoice in this reversion as the way forward to unity, but in actuality one stream has surrendered to the other and forfeited vital elements in the process. It smacks of concession rather than integration. Adjustment has been unilateral. There has been little give and take.

Before closing this brief overview of trends since original publication, we must mention one development which appears to have overridden the issues tackled in this book, bringing charismatics and evangelicals together with a very different agenda —namely, 'revival'. The longing for and expectation of a great new move of God's Spirit, both in the church and the world, has overridden other issues, apparently pushing many of them into a secondary place.

This new preoccupation is an acknowledgement that the churches, both old and new, have failed to stop the moral and spiritual rot in society, or even in their own ranks. This confessed failure has led to sincere intercession – that God himself will and must intervene if there is to be a change in the situation. Some claim precedent in 'old-time' revivals, particularly in the last three centuries. Others believe an 'end-time' revival has been promised as the climax of church history. Some see 'revival' in terms of improving the *quality* of the church, while others see a great increase in *quantity*; perhaps most expect, or at least hope, for both.

Surely, say many, to pray and prepare for 'revival' is far more important and relevant than to discuss our remaining differences. Won't revival resolve these anyway? Won't a sovereign work of God render our divided streams obsolete?

We can easily be carried away by such arguments. But they need to be challenged or we could be distracted from our present and future responsibilities.

Revival has not come yet. In spite of many events which have been hailed as its precursors, the initial drops of a downpour, the cloudburst has not happened, at least in this country (the United Kingdom). Nor is it by any means certain that it is on its way, in spite of 'prophetic' predictions, some of which have already proved to be wishful thinking. Personally, I believe persecution is far more likely to be our future prospect as the 'end' draws nearer.

However, even if the hope is fulfilled, that does not excuse us from our immediate responsibility, part of which is to be the kind of church that can handle a 'revival'. Preparation for such a work of God must surely include repentance and reform according to his word. Why should we expect him to put things right if we are not willing to do the same?

If we are faced with the unfamiliar but welcome problem of a large influx of new converts, they will need to be given the best possible initiation into a worshipping, well-taught and maturing church that combines evangelical convictions and charismatic enthusiasm. The early church had both. So must we.

The publishers and I share the opinion that the message of this volume is still relevant and needed.

J. David Pawson
Sherborne St John
June, 1998

FOREWORD
by
Clive Calver

Former General Secretary, Evangelical Alliance

Twelve years ago I wrote a book to examine the conflict and mutual damage inflicted upon each other by evangelical Christians. It was entitled, *With a Church Like This, Who Needs Satan?* The title and the foreword were provided by David Pawson. It is a genuine delight to be able to return the favour!

David always writes with a penetrating logic. He always attempts to provoke a re-examination of established attitudes. Whatever one's reactions to the conclusions, he is usually successful in that endeavour. This book is no exception, but it is rarely comfortable to look into a mirror and see ourselves. Far easier to examine the image of others.

For Christians have continued to focus on their perceived differences. This is often in the absence of accurate information. It has proved more convenient to concentrate on our own disagreements at the expense of challenging our increasingly secularised society with the truth of the message of Jesus Christ.

Charismatic evangelicals and their non-charismatic counterparts have frequently been most united in their mutual suspicion of one another. For the damage done to our morale has been devastating, and the reduction in credibility which has ensued from our divisions has seriously impaired the effectiveness of our witness and testimony.

An attempt to analyse the grounds for our differences is long overdue. Here, perhaps, lies the prime motive behind this volume. David lucidly probes the theological basis for both charismatic and non-charismatic perspectives. In so doing, he highlights areas of tension with a sensitivity which stimulates the desire to echo Agrippa's assertion to Paul that one would want to hear more on these issues. Instead of exacerbating the problem, David's desire is to enable each to understand the other better.

At a time when there are over one million evangelicals in England alone, it is significant to note that forty-seven per cent claim to be charismatic evangelicals, while fifty-three per cent would prefer to be known as non-charismatic evangelicals. Clearly each needs to be more aware of the opinions of the other. There are also in excess of six thousand Roman Catholics who would term themselves 'charismatic' or 'evangelical'. And that figure is increasing. Here again serious theological work is needed to reflect the opinions they hold. This book begins that investigation, and is welcome indeed.

David's timely words will not meet with universal agreement. Many will feel the need to challenge some of his conclusions. Yet there is an underlying sense of fairness in what he attempts. For when the prime motive behind a work like this is positive, the results will almost inevitably reflect the ground from which they emerge.

It takes a brave man to attempt to make a pathway through a minefield. This is what David Pawson has intended, and although the occasional explosion may ensue in his wake, he has produced a book of great value. The eirenic tone belies the fears some may have in approaching these pages.

Always stimulating, and never afraid to probe tender areas, David's investigation enables the reader to emerge relatively unscathed. But this is only true in terms of terminal damage. Each will suffer from his penetrating critique. Yet few will escape the conclusion that while the bases for disagreement are valid, there is far more to unite evangelicals than to divide them.

Perhaps the time has come to conclude that the word 'evangelical' is most usefully employed as a noun. Adjectives like 'charismatic', 'pseudobaptist' or 'non-charismatic' may be used to qualify the noun. But they cannot replace it. The questions raised for non-evangelical charismatic Catholics are profound, but here again David's logic insists that conclusions must be obtained if unnecessary hurts are to be avoided.

The reader is left to reflect on the fact that, had this book emerged a decade previously, our unity might be stronger than it is today. Certainly our understanding of each other would be better. But the debt we owe to David Pawson would not be greater. For this issue still divides, and a fourth wave may yet be imminent!

October, 1992

PROLOGUE

THE OVERLAPPING CIRCLES

For some decades, charismatics and evangelicals have been drawing closer to each other. The time is ripe for the two fastest growing streams in Christendom to be fully integrated.

This assumes that they are not yet fully together, as this book will reveal. Yet neither are they fully apart. A growing number would use both titles to describe themselves. Some would question whether such a book as this even needs to be written; given time for the present trend to continue, integration is considered inevitable.

The fact is that though the circumferences of these two Christian 'circles' overlap on an increasing scale, the two centres are still separated. While there are many 'charismatic evangelicals', there are still some 'non-charismatic evangelicals' (particularly those whose theology is 'reformed' or 'dispensational') and some 'non evangelical charismatics' (mainly 'Catholic' but some 'liberal').

The difference can be illustrated by asking each group what is their basis of assurance in salvation. Charismatics would talk about the Spirit, evangelicals would point to the scripture. Either might mention the other, but the emphasis would be quite different.

This variation in starting-point affects many areas of the Christian faith and life, the most important of which I have tried to cover here.

My qualification for daring to tackle such controversial themes is that I have personal knowledge and experience of both circles, having been in the overlap for many years. Readers may welcome a little personal information about 'where I'm coming from'.

It was in 1947, just before entering university as an agricultural student, that I discovered the Lord Jesus Christ as a personal Saviour, at Hildenborough Hall, a Christian holiday centre run by a cousin through marriage, Tom Rees. However, this was undoubtedly the fruit of being brought up in a godly home; my father was Professor Cecil Pawson, a widely known lay preacher who became vice-president of the Methodist conference.

Some years later, I switched from farming to 'the' ministry in response to what I believed was a divine call. After serving as a pastor in the Shetland Isles (which until then I had always thought were located in a box in the Firth of Forth!), I trained for the Methodist ministry by reading theology at Cambridge.

It was around 1957, while serving in Arabia as a chaplain in the Royal Air Force, that I became an 'evangelical', independently of any outside influence. Instead of taking texts and topics, I resolved to preach the Bible, the whole Bible and nothing but the Bible. The results convinced me of its inspiration and authority; and its definitive place in my thinking has remained with me. It became my judge in all matters of belief and behaviour.

But this precipitated a crisis on my return to civilian life. My study of scripture had led me to the conclusion that believers' baptism was the only form of the sacrament taught in the New Testament (see my book: *Explaining Water Baptism*, Sovereign World, 1992). I could no longer 'christen' babies. I was expected to resign and did, with good feelings on all sides.

Within hours of terminating my ministry in the Methodist church, I was preparing to become the pastor of the Gold Hill Baptist Church in Chalfont St Peter, Buckinghamshire. The church grew under a Bible-based ministry and I became known on the 'evangelical' circuit, speaking at conventions and conferences.

However, in 1964 I had a decisive experience, again by myself, while praying for a sick deacon, with whom I did not get on very well. I found myself praying fluently in a new language (it sounded like Chinese!). Healing and reconciliation resulted. The following Sunday a member of the congregation, now a Baptist minister in North Wales, asked me after the service: 'What's happened to you this week? You know what you're talking about now!'

So now I was 'charismatic', as well as 'evangelical'. I lost some of my evangelical friends and gained some charismatic ones in their place. Perhaps it was greedy to want both but in those days it often had to be a choice.

Two years later I gave an address on 'Charismatic Gifts' to the National Assembly of Evangelicals in Church House, Westminster. That I was invited to do so was due to the broad-minded and far-sighted General Secretary of the Evangelical Alliance, Gilbert Kirby (his successor and son-in-law, Clive Calver, shares my burden and has generously written the Foreword for this book). It was my first public venture into the heavily mined no-man's land between the two camps.

Much (living) water has flowed under the bridge since then. I have attended and addressed many charismatic conferences. I have recovered most, but not all, of my evangelical relationships and opportunities. I have spoken and written for both streams in many parts of the world, though each has often viewed me as a visitor from the other!

So for many years I have longed and worked for the reconciliation of these two positions: It has been a joy to see mutual fears and suspicions diminish.

Something like a Hegelian dialectic is involved, in which

the solution to the gap between the evangelical thesis and the charismatic antithesis will not be found at some mid-point of 'balance' between them, but in a new synthesis above them both. The outlines of such a synthesis will emerge as we consider its constituent elements.

This book is something of a companion volume, a sequel, to *The Normal Christian Birth* (Hodder and Stoughton, 1989). In that volume, the attempt to synthesise charismatic and evangelical insights was only applied to the single issue of Christian initiation. Chapter 9 in this volume is largely derived from that study and briefly summarises its conclusions (which bear repetition!). The present investigation ranges much more widely, hopefully covering all the issues over which there is still some disagreement.

Some comments are needed to explain the approach used here. The stance taken is from a mid-point, even though that is not the place to which both are invited. It is therefore critical of both positions, appealing to both to engage in self-examination, without which reconciliation is impossible (as every marriage counsellor knows).

This raised the difficult decision as to whether I spoke of them in the first or third person plural. If I referred to each as 'they' and 'them', it could look as if I was disassociating myself from both and was crying: 'a plague on both your houses' in true Shakespearean fashion. If I referred to each as 'we' and 'us', this could be interpreted as patronising, as putting myself forward as the peacemaker. I compromised with 'we' on the original cover and 'they' on the inside pages!

Part I is admittedly one-sided and is mainly an apologia for the charismatics. That is partly because there has been more hostility on the part of evangelicals towards them than vice-versa. And of course, evangelicals have been part of the established scene for much longer and it is the newcomer who has greater difficulty in being accepted. Furthermore, charismatics have not always been very efficient or effective in communicating their position.

Part II balances this up. In each chapter, charismatics are the first subject of my critique, and, in some cases, the worst! Since it is so much easier to see the splinter in someone else's eye than the beam in one's own, it is hoped that each will give greater attention to those sections most relevant to themselves. 'Lord, is it I?' is always a more profitable reaction than 'Lord, that's him alright'.

The inclusion of three appendices requires explanation. Two give a more detailed exegesis of points made in the course of my overall thesis; had they been included in the main text, the reader would have been side-tracked from the flow of thought.

The first examines the purpose behind Paul's letter to the Romans. Most evangelicals assume it is a summary of his, and therefore our, gospel, containing all the basic essentials for evangelism. Since charismatic distinctives are almost totally absent, they are regarded as relatively unimportant.

I seriously question the initial assumption and the inference drawn from it.

The second looks at a notoriously 'difficult' passage in Paul's letter to the Corinthians, in which he appears to contradict himself. Since one sentence, taken out of context, is being used to justify the corporate use of tongues in public worship, even in evangelism, I felt it necessary to expound it more fully.

The final appendix reproduces the address I gave to the National Assembly of Evangelicals in 1966, already referred to. It was reprinted with the other contributions (in *Unity in Diversity*, Evangelical Alliance, 1967); since this is long out of print, I reproduce it here. It adds nothing to my 'case' so may be safely ignored; but I believe it provides an interesting comparison.

There is an obvious contrast between my spoken and written style (I was then speaking from notes and a transcript was made from the recorded tape). There is not much variation between my views then and now (no prizes for spotting them!), though I hope some maturing might be apparent. However, there are two significant changes of emphasis.

One is a shift of interest from exercising the gifts of the Spirit to experiencing the gift of the Spirit (see Chapter 1). This marks a move from pastoral to theological issues, since the latter lie behind the former. In particular, my attention has increasingly focused on the question of initiation into charismatic activity rather than its expression. That is because resistance to its manifestations is considerably reduced. In that respect, my address feels outdated.

The other development is far more important. Whereas then my prime concern was that evangelicals should appreciate and welcome the charismatic contribution, my main burden now is the opposite to this. The charismatic renewal is now widely accepted, particularly in the younger generation, yet is in real need of appreciating and welcoming the evangelical contribution.

A second generation of leaders is emerging, without a solid grounding in scripture. Their contagious enthusiasm is heartening, but without a foundation in the Word, it is vulnerable to both misdirection and burn-out. I spend an increasing amount of my time encouraging them to study and teach the Bible.

My attention was recently drawn to a remarkable 'prophecy' made in 1947, by one of the outstanding 'pentecostal' figures of this century, Smith Wigglesworth, an uneducated Yorkshire plumber who introduced thousands to the person and power of the Holy Spirit, all over the world. A week before his death, he predicted two developments in the universal church. The first would be the restoration of the gifts of the Spirit. The second would be a revived emphasis on the word of God. He added: 'When these two moves of the Spirit combine, we shall see the greatest move the church of Jesus Christ has ever seen' (cited in *Wigglesworth — A Man Who Walked With God*, by George Stormont, Sovereign World, 1989).

Since my manuscript had already been completed, the reader can imagine my feelings when I read these words. I was excited by the promised prospect of the two overlapping circles becoming one, in which the liberty of the Spirit and the light of the scripture would be beautifully blended. I sensed I was touching a desire in the very heart of God. And I was awed by the possibility that this book might play a tiny part in its fulfilment.

We have come a long way towards each other. One final effort could take us there. Yet this last stage of the journey could prove the most difficult. The 'fourth wave' may be the biggest and, like surfers, we must catch it just at the right time and in the right way.

I believe we have reached a critical point. This may be illustrated by the two 'Lausanne' conferences. The first, in 1974, at the city of that name in Switzerland, was almost entirely evangelical in the composition of delegates and the content of declarations. Perhaps its greatest result was the restoration of social action alongside evangelism in evangelical 'mission'. The second, in 1989, at Manila in the Philippines, was still evangelical on the platform (with one or two exceptions) but quite different on the 'floor'. The large proportion of 'third world' participants meant that many, if not most, were charismatic evangelicals. The discrepancy led to moments of tension which were not always satisfactorily resolved. This sounded the death-knell of evangelical indifference towards charismatics. It would seem impossible to hold a third Lausanne conference, if that is felt desirable or necessary, unless and until the differences are honestly reviewed and resolved.

May this volume help us to do just that, for Christ's sake.

Amen.

PART I

THE DIFFERENCES
REVIEWED

1

WHAT IS A 'CHARISMATIC'?

Almost unheard of fify years ago, the label is now applied so freely that it has a number of different meanings.

It is used of *some unbelievers*. From pop stars to presidents, public figures are said to have 'got it', whatever 'it' is. The impression is that they possess a strong personal magnetism which attracts fans and followers. They have 'appeal'.

That is not the meaning in this book, though it has to be admitted that the church is not entirely free from its 'star' performers who can draw the crowds!

It is used of *all believers*. In a television interview, George Carey, then Archbishop of Canterbury, was asked if he was a 'charismatic' and replied: 'All Christians are. The term comes from the Greek word *charis*, which means grace. All Christians have received the grace of God.'

While there is an element of truth in this wide definition,

it does not reflect the popular usage, even in church circles. Indeed, the interviewer immediately added: 'I meant – do you speak in tongues?' (to which the Archbishop responded: 'I think I once did, many years ago'). But this definition is too narrow.

It is usually used of *some believers* to distinguish them from others. So what is it that makes them different? Is it their behaviour or their belief? Many would use the word to describe a certain style of behaviour that is increasingly apparent in Christian meetings for worship and fellowship – more informal, even casual, with plenty of action (hands and feet) to lots of music (guitars and drums rather than organs or pianos), accompanied by expressions of mutual love (hugs and kisses all round).

But while much of this was introduced by what has been called the 'charismatic renewal', there are cultural factors involved. Many of the features belong to the youth culture and are infiltrating all streams of church life.

Belief, none the less, underlies behaviour. It would be a mistake to confuse the fruit with the root. In charismatic circles, as in others, conduct sprang from convictions. At the heart of the 'renewal' lay two deeply held beliefs. We shall now consider these in detail.

THE GIFT OF THE SPIRIT IS TO BE EXPERIENCED

The two greatest gifts of God to us are the gift of his Son (John 3:16) and the gift of his Spirit (Acts 2:38). Gifts need to be received. How is the Spirit received?

Charismatics believe this 'reception' is a definite event, clearly discernible to the recipient and others present at the time. Essentially an inward experience, it is accompanied by outward evidence, both audible and visible (Acts 2:33).

The book of Acts plays a considerable part in this thinking. The experiences recorded there are taken as a norm. There is no hesitation in using the same language, which is rich in synonyms. Such phrases as 'baptised in the Spirit' and 'filled with the Spirit' (or the equivalent, 'Spirit-baptism' and 'Spirit-filled') are freely used by charismatics; though other biblical descriptions, like 'fallen upon' or 'poured out', are less common among them.

Some would limit the evidence to speaking in tongues (i.e. other languages unknown to the speaker). Others would not insist on this particular manifestation. All would expect clear indication that the Spirit had been given and received.

THE GIFTS OF THE SPIRIT ARE TO BE EXERCISED

Charismatics believe and expect that the experience of the gift will lead to the exercise of the gifts. The reception of supernatural power releases supernatural abilities. These are to be distinguished from natural abilities, possessed by unbelievers before conversion and dedicated to the Lord after coming to faith. The world can receive neither the 'gift of the Spirit' (John 14:17; Acts 2:38) nor his gifts. They are unique to believers, though they can be confused with fleshly substitutes or demonic counterfeits.

The twelfth chapter of Paul's first letter to the Corinthians figures prominently in charismatic thinking. It is one of the clearest lists of these special gifts and leads on to the fullest exposition of their use.

While all the 'gifts' are believed to have been available to the whole church for the whole of her history on earth, some are more prominent, or at least more frequent, in charismatic circles today. Prophecy, tongues and healing tend to dominate the scene.

* * * * *

These two basic principles, experiencing the gift and exercising the gifts, belong together, complement one another and, when properly combined, provide a remarkable balance in understanding life in the Spirit, which is both individual and corporate.

The initial reception is by each, but the continuing supply is for all (Gal 3:2, 5). The first gift is often tongues (to edify one's self); the others are all to be given away to others (to edify the 'body'). The single filling needs to be followed by repeated fillings or continual 'fullness' (Acts 2:4; 4:31; Eph 5:18).

Both these beliefs are very practical, immediately affecting outward behaviour and achieving real results, which are clearly apparent to the senses. Though faith precedes them, sight follows.

Together, they constitute proof of divine activity. They 'confirm' both acceptance by God of the person and the presence of God among his people.

The intimate connection between the two needs to be emphasised. That is because there is a growing readiness to accept the second (exercise of the gifts) and a growing reluctance to accept the first (experience of the gift).

Objective observers have noted that only where the 'baptism' is clearly offered and experienced are the 'gifts' manifested on a significant scale. A full 'charismatic' recognises this integral link, convinced that one leads to the other, that both are to be preached and practised.

This, then, is the sense in which the term is being used throughout this volume. It is obvious that, defined in this way, the label cannot be attached to all professing Christians. It is one stream among others, but it is a growing one and it runs through most denominations.

Of course, not all who call themselves 'charismatic' would identify with the definition presented here. After reading this book, some may wonder whether they are correct in describing themselves in this way. Hopefully, many others will be more confident to do so.

Was there ever a time when the whole church was 'charismatic'? The record of church history is not as negative as some would imagine, as we shall see. For the most part, however, it has to be admitted that the evidence is scanty. However, there is one period during which the claim might be substantiated – namely, the first few decades, of which we have a record in the New Testament. If this were established, that would carry more significance than all later centuries for those who regard scripture as normative. To that investigation we now turn.

2

WERE THERE CHARISMATICS IN THE NEW TESTAMENT?

Certainly, no one used the label, either of themselves or others. And they fought hard against anything that smacked of 'party' spirit and the threat of factions.

So the exact word is nowhere to be found. The nearest would be *charismata*, translating into English as 'spiritual gifts' (1 Cor 12:1; note that the context applies this word to 'each' and every church member). 'Charismatic' is, in fact, an adjectival derivation from this very noun. But that could limit its application to only one of the two basic principles outlined in the previous chapter.

What we are asking is whether the experience of the gift as well as the exercise of the gifts was widespread, even universal, in the early church. It will be helpful to distinguish three phases of the Spirit's activity during this period – before, during and after the coming of Jesus, the Christ, the Messiah. His advent marked a clear change; indeed, it made possible what had only been prophetic promises up till then.

PRE-MESSIANIC

The birth of Jesus was preceded by a surge of the Holy Spirit's activity. This mainly consisted of prophecies and other special revelations (often through dreams), together with miracles. Supernatural messengers (angels) play a major part. Such happenings had been virtually unknown for nearly four centuries.

Zechariah was struck dumb for doubting his elderly wife's pregnancy, though his tongue was released into prophecy when the baby was born. Their son John was filled with the Spirit before he was born and began his ministry of publicising the messianic advent while still a six-month foetus! Though he did no miracles, he reactivated the prophetic ministry which had been silent so long.

The Spirit 'came on' Mary, enabling her to conceive without fertilisation – and a boy at that (ovaries can only produce female eggs). In her submission to this supernatural act of creation by the power of the Spirit, with all its consequences, many (particularly Roman Catholics) see her as the model charismatic. She also prophesied – in what the liturgy calls 'The Magnificat' (from its opening words in Luke 1:46) . Yet there is no record of her particular 'reception' of the Spirit; it may even be that the first 'evidence' was a missed period. However, she did later share in Pentecost and spoke in tongues with the rest (Acts 1:14; 2:1); though that appears to mark the end of her special ministry rather than its beginning, for that is the last mention of her name.

Joseph received words of knowledge and wisdom in dreams (does this indicate he was much older than Mary? Joel 2:28). There is no record of him speaking such words (or even any words, for that matter!).

Simeon and Anna did speak; he is recorded prophesying and she is described as a prophetess. Both had the gift of discernment to recognise the fulfilment of God's purpose of the ages in a tiny baby.

Two things may be noticed about all this 'charismatic' activity. First, most of it is recorded by Luke in his gospel – the same author who wrote the book of Acts. It is clear that he had an interest in this dimension and saw both continuity and connection between his two volumes. Equally significant is his very close link with the apostle Paul.

Second, while there is clearly exercise of the gifts, there is no record of any experience of the gift in this pre-messianic phase, no obvious occasion on which the Spirit was 'received'. This is very much in line with the pattern of the Spirit's activity in the Old Testament. He came on some of the people from time to time for direct and immediate purposes of ministry (Samson is a good example in Judges 13–16).

The prophets (particularly Ezekiel and Joel) foresaw a time when the Spirit would be given to all God's people as a permanent possession for continuous ministry. This would involve an initial gift as well as inspired gifts. This new pattern was inaugurated with Jesus.

MESSIANIC

Jesus' entry into his ministry, at the age of thirty, became a model for the age of the church, the 'new age' of the Spirit.

Significantly, his *experience of the gift* took place immediately after his baptism in water and in response to his prayer (Luke 3:21f). There was visible and audible evidence of the event – both a dove and a voice came down from heaven. The Spirit 'descended and came to rest *upon* him' (the preposition is prominent in his first sermon at Nazareth, where the verb 'anointed' is also used, as it was later by Peter to describe this occasion; Luke 4:18; cf Acts 10:38).

To his cousin John 'the baptiser', this evidence had a twofold significance. Not only had Jesus been thus designated the Messiah, the 'Anointed One' (Ps 2:2), he would be the one to pass on the anointing to others, he would 'baptise (immerse) them in the Holy Spirit', as clearly and definitely as he and the others had been baptised (immersed) in water (John 1:33; note that Jesus himself is here given the same title as John: 'the baptiser').

His *exercise of the gifts* followed, though not immediately. Prophecy was the most prominent, causing many to speculate whether he was *the* prophet foretold by Moses (John 6:14; 7:40; cf Deut 18:15). Indeed, he never spoke except in prophecy (John 7:16; 8:28)!

The most public gifts were healing and miracles. The lame walked, the blind saw, the deaf heard, the dead were raised, water was made into wine. Even the historical references to Jesus outside canonical scripture describe him as a 'wonder worker'.

His discernment of spirits is evident when dealing with the Gadarene demoniac, his faith in stilling the storm and cursing the fig-tree, the word of knowledge in talking to Nathaniel or the Samaritan woman, the word of wisdom in his answer to questions like taxation by Caesar.

So all the gifts were manifest in this one body (as they would later be in his other body, the church). The only one not specifically mentioned is that of tongues. This silence does not prove he didn't (or did) pray or praise in this way; we have no record of any of his private prayers. One could speculate that his communion with his Father was such as not to need this aid, for that is its main purpose. That he later gave this gift to others, and that it enabled them to speak in his very language, is indisputable (Acts 2:32; Rom 8:15; Gal 4:6).

We conclude that, according to our definition, Jesus was 'charismatic'.

POST-MESSIANIC

The *twelve apostles* were to undergo a radical change in their relationship with the Spirit.

The first phase, during the three years' public ministry of Jesus, which included Judas, experienced both the power and the presence of the Spirit *with* them – though they did not realise his personhood, were not conscious of his activity and the anointing was intermittent. This, again, was more like the Old Testament pattern and quite unlike that of Jesus himself, who had received the Spirit 'without limit' (John 3:34). However, Jesus predicted a change in this situation that would bring them into line with himself. The Spirit who had been *with* them would be *in* them and *stay* with them (John 14:16f).

The second phase, which excluded Judas and included Matthias, began on the day of Pentecost with their experience of the gift, for which Jesus had told them to wait before attempting any more ministry in his name (Luke 24:49). There was both audible and visible evidence that they had 'received' (note Peter's 'see and hear' in Acts 2:33). The range of vocabulary used to describe what happened is interesting: 'baptised in, rest on, filled with, poured out on, came on' (Acts 1:5; 2:3f, 17; 11:15).

This led to gifts, the first being tongues. Soon there would be healings (a forty-year-old lame beggar) and miracles (the raising of Dorcas). Prophetic revelations in the form of visions and dreams, words of knowledge and wisdom, as well as signs and wonders, accompanied the apostolic ministry.

We conclude that the twelve apostles, with Matthias substituted for Judas, were all 'charismatic'.

Paul may also be included. Three days after his encounter with the ascended Lord Jesus, he was baptised in water and filled with Holy Spirit through the laying-on of hands by Ananias. The outward sign was release from blindness, but it may be that his regular use of tongues began at this point. The combination of baptism in water and reception of Spirit was not the only parallel with Jesus; it was also followed by a solitary period in the wilderness.

His later ministry was replete with spiritual gifts. He claimed to speak in tongues more than all the Corinthian believers put together, though primarily in his private devotions. His message was confirmed with signs and wonders, as with the other apostles (Acts 14:3; Rom 15:18f; 1 Thess 1:5). He blinded a man (as he himself had been blinded!), he handled a snake, he raised the dead. Words of knowledge and wisdom poured from his lips. He needed and exercised discernment of spirits (Acts 13:9; 16:18).

So far we have demonstrated that 'the twelve' and 'thirteenth' ('last of all'; 1 Cor 15:8) apostles were all 'charismatic'. Most Bible students readily acknowledge this. But what about the other prominent figures in the early church and what about the thousands of unnamed 'ordinary' members, described as 'believers', 'brethren' or 'disciples'? Did they also experience the gift and exercise the gifts?

The *early believers* were 'one in heart and mind . . . they shared everything they had' (Acts 5:32). Did their 'fellowship' (*koinonia*) in the Spirit extend to participation in the apostles' charismatic experience? The evidence points that way.

We can begin with the day of Pentecost itself. From the beginning others shared in what happened to the apostles – one hundred and eight others to be precise. Furthermore, when Peter preached, he promised that those who responded to his message would 'receive' the same 'gift' just given to himself and his companions (Acts 2:38), since the 'promise' (Luke 24:49; Acts 2:39) was in no way limited, except by the failure to repent when called by God. Clearly, Peter expected many others to be baptised in or filled with Holy Spirit in the same way as he had.

Sure enough, the book of Acts records a number of such incidents. The next is at Samaria, where those who responded to Philip's preaching by repenting, believing and being baptised later 'received' Holy Spirit through the laying-on of hands by Peter and John. Though the outward sign that the gift had been given and received is not specified on this occasion, it was clear enough for Simon to want to be an agent of such an impressive display.

The next is at Caesarea, where a Roman centurion and his household received the gift before Peter finished preaching!

When he later defended his action of eating with Gentiles and baptising them, Peter expressly claimed that their 'reception' of the Spirit was exactly the same as his own and was a fulfilment of the promise of Jesus to the apostles (Acts 11:15–17). Tongues and praise were the outward evidence on this occasion.

The fourth and last such event to be recorded in Acts took place at Ephesus among some followers of John the baptiser, who had been taught by Apollos that the Jewish scriptures proved Jesus to be the Messiah. Assuming (wrongly, as it turned out) that this knowledge indicated full Christian faith, yet puzzled by the apparent lack of normal Christian life, Paul asked when, or even if, they had received the Spirit, clearly appealing to the memory of their experience rather than checking the orthodoxy of their doctrine. On discovering that their real repentance had not been matched with full faith, he introduced them to a deeper understanding of Christ, baptised them as believers into his name, then laid hands on them, at which point the Spirit came on them, again with the outward expression of tongues, this time accompanied by prophesying.

In every case, the reception of the Spirit was a conscious experience with clear evidence. In no case was it purely internal, much less unconscious. It was 'a definite fact concerning which they could name the time and place', to quote one biblical scholar. In his epistles, Paul frequently appealed to the recollection of the happening in his readers (e.g. 1 Cor 12:13; Gal 3:2; Tit 3:5).

There is also considerable evidence that the exercise of gifts was widespread in the early church and not limited to the apostles. Stephen, a 'deacon' chosen to serve tables, 'did great wonders and miraculous signs among the people' (Acts 6:8). Agabus, Philip and his four daughters have the ministry of prophecy. Ananias heals the blind Saul. Even the Corinthians, for all their theological and ethical confusion, 'do not lack any spiritual gift' (1 Cor 1:7). The Galatians witnessed continual miracles (Gal 3:5). If the last part of Mark's gospel (16:9–20) is, as many scholars think, an addition by the early church, then it reflects a situation in which speaking in tongues, healing the sick and casting out demons were normal activities.

* * * * *

However, all these indications are not always considered sufficient evidence that the entire New Testament church was 'charismatic', as we have defined the term. Two major objections to this interpretation of the data have been made, questioning whether it can in any way be regarded as a norm for today.

The *experience of the gift* has been challenged by pointing out that there are only four instances of a 'pentecostal' reception, which is statistically inadequate to establish a universal pattern.

Furthermore, in each of these instances the persons

concerned were the first representatives of a new category of people —Jews (in Acts 2), Samaritans (in Acts 8), Gentiles (in Acts 10), disciples of John (in Acts 19). This last, of course, does not quite fit the series (if that is based on the order in Acts 1:8); but it was a unique group which, inevitably in the course of time, would tend to decline and disappear.

The argument is that the four 'pentecosts' are abnormal rather than normal, special happenings to mark the ever-widening citizenship of the kingdom and membership of the church. Repetition of such unique occurrences should not be expected.

However, it does not follow that because these groups were 'special' (only in the sense of being the first of their 'kind'), what happened to them was different from what happened to everyone else. It could just as easily be argued that these four incidents were recorded precisely because the *same* experience was now shared by *different* people, the normal was now given to those who hitherto would not have been regarded as eligible. There is evidence to show that this is the right interpretation.

This can be highlighted by asking a simple question: how did anyone *know* that the Samaritans had not received the Spirit (Acts 8:16)? They had repented, believed, been baptised and were full of joy – yet Holy Spirit had not yet 'come on' them. The phrase gives the answer to our question: there had been no 'pentecostal' manifestation. But the conclusion that this omission meant the gift had not been received clearly implies that such experience was normal, even universal, for *all believers up to that time*. This was the first occasion on which it had not occurred, hence the apostles' concern. Scholars have speculated as to *why* there was a delay; most conclude, probably rightly, that the Lord was thus establishing unity between Samaritan and Jewish believers. But they miss the real point that the Samaritan believers were abnormal in *not* experiencing the gift in a 'pentecostal' manner!

Similarly, Peter sees in the experience of Cornelius' household not only a mirror of his own at Pentecost, but also that of the brethren in Joppa (note the 'we' in Acts 10:47) and all the brethren in Jerusalem (note the 'us' in Acts 15:8).

Was this what Paul missed in the Ephesian 'disciples'? Certainly, he enquired whether they had 'received Holy Spirit' (Acts 19:2). In his letters to different churches he uses 'pentecostal' terms for this experience: 'receive' (Gal 3:2), 'baptised in' (1 Cor 12:13), 'poured out on' (Tit 3:5).

There is a noticeable reluctance to use such terms among those who limit the experience of the gift to the 'abnormal' occasion, though the New Testament applies them indiscriminately to all believers. The onus of proof would seem to rest on those taking this view, rather than on those who regard the biblical examples of receiving Holy Spirit as the norm.

The *exercise of the gifts* has been challenged by the claim that such extraordinary abilities were only needed to attest the apostles' oral teaching until it could take written form and would then be rendered obsolete. Once the New Testament 'canon' (the collection of apostolic documents which would be the 'rule' for the church in matters of belief and behaviour) was complete and approved, the spiritual gifts would disappear.

Appeal is made to Paul's teaching that prophecy, tongues and knowledge will 'pass away' (1 Cor 13:8–13). But this is the only passage in which this is said and a careful study of the context gives a time reference that is still future – when perfection comes and the Lord is seen face to face. This can hardly refer to the writing of scripture.

It is also difficult to understand the logical necessity of attestation for the direct oral transmission of the gospel by the apostles and its irrelevance to the less direct written form. Certainly, such an incredible message requires divine confirmation and the New Testament confirms that this took place, not just when the apostles spoke (Heb 2:4; though even this is ambiguous and could refer to others) but also when ordinary 'disciples' communicated their faith (Mark 16:20).

Furthermore, this thinking demands an arbitrary division of various lists of gifts and ministries in the New Testament (for example, in Romans 12:6–8, where all but prophecy are accepted as continuing; in 1 Corinthians 14:26, where hymns and words of instruction are 'in', but tongues and interpretation are 'out'; or Ephesians 4:11, where evangelists, pastors and teachers are accepted but apostles and prophets are rejected). Such selectivity seems quite subjective, with no ground for the discrimination in scripture itself.

While tradition does not carry the authority of scripture, it is at least relevant to ask whether in fact the gifts did die out at the end of the apostolic era or whether they continued, with more or less frequency, throughout church history. It seems better to keep that quest for the next chapter, since this one has been concerned with that period covered by scripture and therefore carrying more authority than later developments in church life.

3

HAS THE CHURCH ALWAYS BEEN CHARISMATIC?

History was my second worst subject in school ('Scripture knowledge' earned me even lower marks!), probably because I found it so boring, though I think the teacher was partly responsible. I could see no point in it.

Now I'm fascinated with history, since I can now see where it's all going and how God is working out his purposes in time. I am even more interested in church history, though it often leads me to the conclusion of the 'Teacher', that 'there is nothing new under the sun' (Ecc 1:9). The answer to many of our current ecclesiastical problems lies in the past.

Yet most church historians never mention any charismatic dimension of church life. Either consciously or unconsciously they have ignored this aspect, leaving the impression that there were no such experiences for the major part of the last two thousand years.

When this silence was linked to the belief that supernatural gifts were limited to the time of the apostles, there seemed to be no reason for historians to think about them at all, except perhaps to complete records of the earliest days for the archives.

Unfortunately, I am not a historian, having neither the ability nor the opportunity to indulge in the necessary research. I rely on reading the works of others for my knowledge of the life of the church through the ages. So I invite you to come and browse with me in my library (three tonnes of books, according to the last furniture remover!).

We are seeking an answer to the question: did the 'baptism' and 'gifts' of the Spirit die with the apostles, much later or even at all?

Professor Ronald Kydd, in *Charismatic Gifts in the Early Church* (Hendrickson, 1984), finds clear evidence of their use in the *Didache* (otherwise known as 'The Teaching of the Twelve Apostles'), the writings of Clement of Rome, Ignatius, Hermas (the 'Shepherd'), Justin Martyr, Celsus, Irenaeus, Eusebius of Caesarea, Theodotus, Hippolytus, Novatian, Tertullian, Cyprian, Origen, Dionysius, Firmilian. He also finds indirect testimony in the Odes of Solomon and the Apocryphal Book of Acts. He investigates the fringe sect led by Montanus, one of whose aims was to see the gifts restored to a central place – though they tended to be led astray by untested prophecies, as others have been since.

It is an impressive array of evidence, which includes

many of the leading figures in the early church. One fact clearly emerges – the gifts did not die with the apostles. Dr Kydd concludes that the gifts remained very important to the church throughout the first and second centuries: 'the church prior to AD 200 was charismatic'. However, in the third century doubts about them began in the Latin-speaking West and we hear only of 'traces' (Cyprian's word) in the Greek-speaking East. He concludes: 'There came a point around AD 260 at which they no longer fitted in the highly organised, well-educated, wealthy, socially powerful Christian communities. The church did not lose its soul, but it did lose those special moments when God broke into the lives of men and women.'

A book by two Catholic scholars covers the same period, this time looking for evidence of the experience of the baptism rather than the exercise of the gifts (*Christian Initiation and Baptism in the Holy Spirit* by Kilian McDonnel and George Montague, Liturgical Press, 1991) and includes an equally impressive list of names: Tertullian, Hilary of Poitiers, Cyril of Jerusalem, John Chrysostom, Philoxenus. They also include the Apostolic Constitutions and some intriguing material from the Syrian or 'Syriac' Christians. They demonstrate a profound link between Spirit-baptism, and water-baptism throughout the period studied, beginning with Jesus' own experience (though this insight is somewhat marred by its assumed transfer to the later rite of infant baptism). The key point for our purpose is that there is clear evidence of an experience of the Spirit into the *fifth* century (when it was called the 'third birth', somewhat akin to the modern 'second blessing'). The exercise of 'charisms' was expected to follow the 'baptism'.

These two studies might seem to support the idea that gifts died out when the 'canon' of scripture was completed in the fourth century (though the books had, of course, been recognised and used long before that). But it would need to be established that there was a necessary link between the two events. Was it the 'closing' of applications for inclusion in the New Testament that caused, or at least led to, the cessation of charismatic activity? Or was it that these two developments merely coincided, along with many other radical changes in church life over that period? Many factors were at work in the fourth and fifth centuries, not least the 'establishment' of Christianity by the Emperor Constantine, after his conversion. It is debatable whether this was a triumph or a tragedy, whether it took the church into the world or brought the world into the church.

Actually, we do not need to speculate. The fact is that the baptism and gifts did *not* die out then, though it has to be admitted that they became more spasmodic, at least as far as the records go. And there is always the possibility that the evidence is far from complete; a church that had become 'respectable' would not want to draw attention to such things.

I visited a new Catholic church centre in Cardigan,

Wales, attracted by its architecture (one of my 'hobbies' is designing church buildings). On its bookstall was a Catholic Truth Society booklet about St David of Wales, which I bought, since I bear the same name and was in the area where he ministered. When he was chosen to be bishop, in the sixth century, he desired to be consecrated in the 'holy city' of Jerusalem, perhaps thinking this would add a special dimension to his ministry. He set off on foot for the pilgrimage (no Jumbo jets in those days!), with a few monks as companions, one of whom kept a journal of their travels. But they had gone only as far as Gaul (France) when, 'ye holy father David was baptised in ye Holy Ghost and spake in tongues as in ye days of ye apostles'.

Some months later I was in the Anglican cathedral in Liverpool, looking at some of its 'treasures' in a glass case. Among them was a hand-written life of St David of Wales, open at a page describing some of the miracles he performed, including the restoring of sight to a blind boy and the healing of an elderly man on his death-bed.

Whenever I am in Wales, I take an unholy glee in telling them that Welsh pentecostalism began long before the 'revival' at the beginning of this century! Would that the recollection of David's experience was featured as prominently as daffodils on March 1st.

I came across a remarkable reprint of a lecture given to the British Medical Association in 1983 by Rex Gardner, a consultant obstetrician and gynaecologist at Sunderland

District General Hospital. The title of his lecture, now in the *British Medical Journal* says it all — 'Miracles of healing in Anglo-Celtic Northumbria as recorded by the Venerable Bede and his contemporaries: a reappraisal in the light of twentieth century experience'. He points out that in this first English church historian's account of the life of Cuthbert of Lindisfarne (Holy Island, off the coast of Northumberland), the miraculous element is so prevalent that if it is excluded, only six out of forty-six chapters remain. He then cites parallel healings associated with modern charismatic fellowships to discourage the dismissal of Bede's records as myths or legends and dares to include contemporary accounts of raising the dead.

In passing, he mentions Augustine's healing of a blind girl in Kent, an event to which Pope Gregory's response was not encouraging. He describes the 'first breath of the modern pentecostal movement' in Monkwearmouth, in 1907, and in a parish church; and notes that five churches of different denominations, all near his home, are all 'charismatic'. It must have taken considerable courage to deliver the lecture!

Through the Middle Ages, there was perhaps too much belief in the supernatural and its expression in miraculous gifts. When this became associated with shrines and relics, the way was open for superstition to replace faith. But it would be as wrong to reject all the accounts as to accept them all. The gift of discernment is needed.

The wonders associated with that remarkable man Francis

of Assisi have led a number of writers to claim him for the true charismatic succession. Not least of the signs was an outburst of musical praise, which usually marks a move of the Spirit.

Among many accounts of raising the dead, we single out two Spanish examples – one by a nun (now known as St Teresa, 1515–1582) and the other by an explorer in the 'new world', who had a miraculous ministry among the Texan Indians (Alvar Muñez Cabeza de Vaca).

Since my purpose in this chapter is not to give an exhaustive survey, but simply to demonstrate that the charismatic dimension did not disappear, we shall jump a few centuries to what became known as 'the eighteenth-century revival', under the ministries of George Whitefield and the Wesley brothers.

A collection of John Wesley's writings on our subject has recently been published in a modern English paraphrase by Clare Weakley (*The Holy Spirit and Power*, Logos International, 1977). Extracts from his journal, sermons and letters leave us in no doubt that Wesley would have welcomed the current charismatic renewal and been very much a part of it.

Most Methodists are only too familiar with his conversion at 8.45 p.m. on May 24th, 1738, at a meeting in Aldersgate Street in London (a plaque on Barclays Bank marks the spot). Significantly, it was while Luther's preface to his commentary on Romans was being read that he knew with joy that he was personally included in Christ's atoning death.

Alas, few know of what happened on January 1st, 1739, in Fetter Lane. Let him speak for himself:

At about three in the morning, as we were continuing in prayer, the power of God came mightily upon us. Many cried out in complete joy. Others were knocked to the ground. As soon as we recovered a little from that awe and amazement at God's presence, we broke out in praise.

The result was that 'the Holy Spirit began to move among us with amazing power when we met in his name'. When anyone fell down under the preaching, they were prayed for until they were 'filled with the peace and joy of the Holy Spirit', which was frequently 'received in a moment'. His journal is full of such accounts. One Quaker who objected to such goings on 'went down as thunderstruck' and rose to cry aloud: 'Now I know you are a prophet of the Lord'. Wesley concluded: 'Similar experiences continued to increase as I preached. It seemed prudent to preach and write on the work of the Holy Spirit'.

Chapter 7 in Weakley's book is entitled 'Gifts of the Holy Spirit' and is extracted from a lengthy letter to Dr Conyers Middleton, dated January 7th, 1749. He had publicly criticised the gifts of the Spirit and Wesley 'soon saw what occasion that good man had given to the enemies of God to blaspheme'.

After citing Justin Martyr, Irenaeus, Theophilus, Tertullian,

Minutius Felix, Origen, Cyprian, Arnobius and Lactantius as evidence that the gifts were not limited to the apostolic age, he gives his own understanding of why they did not remain 'common in the church for more than two or three centuries'. He blamed Constantine for:

heaping riches, power and honour upon Christians in general, but in particular upon the Christian clergy. From that time, the gifts of the Holy Spirit almost totally ceased. . . . The real cause of the loss was that the love of many, almost all the so-called Christians had grown cold . . . So, when this faith and holiness were nearly lost, dry, formal, orthodox men began even then to ridicule whatever gifts they did not have themselves. They belittled and discredited all the gifts of the Spirit as either madness or fraud. As a result, the miraculous gifts of the Holy Spirit were soon withdrawn from the early church.

Wesley goes on to a very positive discussion of raising the dead (he himself raised one Thomas Merick), healing the sick, casting out devils, prophesying and tongues. Regarding historical records of the church, he castigates those who conclude that 'what is not recorded was not done' which is 'by no means a self-evident maxim'. There has been deliberate suppression of those believers who exercised these gifts; he gives the example of tongues-speaking among the Huguenots in France, put down so cruelly by Louis XIV.

I have quoted Wesley at length because this dimension of his thought and life, which was a major factor in the eighteenth century revival, has been widely ignored, even among Methodists; I know this from personal experience.

Moving on to the nineteenth century, there is some interesting information in a paperback, written by Hugh Black, entitled, *The Clash of Tongues with Glimpses of Revival* (New Dawn, 1988). Drawing on another publication (*Speaking in Other Tongues: A Scholarly Defense*, by Barnett and McGregor), he cites three famous evangelicals of the nineteenth century.

An English woman heard the evangelist C. G. Finney pray in an unknown tongue during family devotions; he assured her it was a special gift God had given him. Behind it lay an experience which he described as follows: 'I received a mighty baptism in the Holy Ghost . . . I wept aloud with joy and love; and I do not know but I should say, I literally bellowed out the unutterable gushings of my heart'.

Both in Dallas and London, the American evangelist Dwight L. Moody got up to preach but found himself speaking to the amazed congregation in a strange tongue. Only after spending a little time in prayer and praise in this new language was he able to preach again in English. In one of his last sermons in Boston he declared: 'I believe Pentecost was but a specimen day. I think the church has made this woeful mistake that Pentecost was a miracle that is not to be repeated.' After one of his meetings in England, a number of young men gathered in the local YMCA. An observer recorded: 'I found the meeting on fire. The young men were speaking in tongues and prophesying. What on earth did it all mean? Only that Moody had been addressing them that afternoon.'

Even that 'prince of preachers', Charles Haddon Spurgeon, who packed the huge Metropolitan Tabernacle with Londoners eager to hear what he had to say, told his congregation that when he got especially happy in the Lord, 'I break forth into a kind of gibberish which I do not myself understand'.

When we come to the twentieth century, there is much documentation to choose from.

The first half of the century is dominated by the rise of pentecostalism outside the ranks of traditional denominations. One of the most readable and comprehensive accounts is *The Pentecostal Movement*, by a Norwegian scholar, Nils Bloch-Hoell (Allen and Unwin, 1964; the date is significant). This takes a world-wide perspective, but there are now regional histories available (for example, covering Australia by Barry Chant and New Zealand by James Worsfold). The phenomenal rise of this 'third force in Christendom', well on its way to becoming the 'first' in Latin America and elsewhere, is so well documented and widely known that we need not linger, since our purpose is not to present such a history, but simply establish the continuation of charismatic phenomena.

The second half of the century witnessed the unexpected penetration of 'pentecostalism' into all the mainline churches, to the amazement of many and the consternation of some.

For the moving account of one man's contribution to this remarkable development, read David du Plessis's *The Spirit Bade Me Go*. In 1981 the World Council of Churches in Geneva published a collection of documents, edited by Arnold Bittlinger, called *The Church is Charismatic*, a title that would have been inconceivable even ten years earlier, though its claim is debatable!

Whatever happened during the intervening centuries, the baptism and gifts of the Spirit which characterised the first century have reappeared on an unprecedented scale. It has become virtually impossible to claim they are irrelevant and obsolete, though some still try to do so. Of course, they are then forced to find an alternative explanation for what is happening and must choose between a psychological or a demonic cause. They could increasingly find themselves 'out on a limb', since 'pentecostal' and 'charismatic' Christians will soon be in the majority, particularly in the 'two-thirds' world, as the 'third world' is now called because of its proportion of the population (and of believers).

Before leaving the library, there is another section which is relevant to our quest— biography. Studying the lives of well-known 'saints', past and present, reveals that many of them have experienced the baptism and exercised the gifts without realising what was happening or, in some cases, reluctant to describe it in 'charismatic' terms. Let me pick just one example from the shelf: *Francis Schaeffer: The Man and his Message* by L.G. Parkhurst (Kingsway, 1985).

He is described here, and by many others, as a 'prophet' for our age. I believe that is a valid label for his remarkable ministry, to which I, with thousands of others, owe more than words can express. He opened our eyes to see contemporary culture and the alien philosophy behind it through God's eyes. He was a 'seer' and saw what was really going on in the world more clearly than most others.

How and when was this prophetic gift and ministry released? I found the answer in this biography. It happened in a hayloft in Champéry (well, Christianity began in a stable!). It was here that Schaeffer found himself 'praising God; he began to "feel" songs of praise well up from within himself. He began to sing and write poetry again.' His biographer concludes that:

> The result of Fran's walk in the hayloft of Chalet Bijou really did mark the turning point in his ministry. From the time of that walk in 1951, God began leading the Schaeffers both through the teaching of this Word *and* experientially. . . . he began to insist, in a way that not many were ready to hear, that both reformation and revival were needed in the church.

If that is not 'prophetic', what is?

Yet in spite of this he found the word 'charismatic', and everything associated with it, repugnant. We had some long and deep personal conversations, but this was one of those areas on which we 'agreed to differ'. I think it was because he was so afraid of the 'non-rational', the 'existential', what he called 'upper-storey experiences' that were purely subjective, that to embrace the charismatic renewal would open the door to all that he was fighting against with such zeal. That he was absolutely right about some of its aspects, I have no doubt; but I believe it was wrong to eschew all of it.

I have included Schaeffer because he represents many evangelicals about whom I have read or to whom I have spoken who have had a very real charismatic experience, but who are extremely reluctant, for one reason or another, to recognise or describe it in these terms. In other words, the movement is probably much wider than those who are happy to be thought of as part of it.

Does terminology matter all that much? Why not simply rejoice in the work of the Spirit in all such people without trying to 'claim' it with particular labels?

Certainly, it makes little difference to the people themselves, however they describe their experience. The gifts have been released in them and are being used for others.

The difficulty comes when seeking to release others into similar ministry. The problem becomes acute in finding successors to continue the work. Can others have the same experience and receive the same gift? Can either be 'passed on'? Can the roots of a gifted ministry be conveyed to others, as well as the fruits?

Any attempt to re-duplicate our own experience in the lives

of others can be futile, even dangerous, *unless* there is clear scriptural basis and warrant for doing so. If our experience can be identified with a scriptural promise and that promise is made to all believers, we can confidently offer it to others (which is precisely what Peter was doing on the day of Pentecost; Acts 2:39).

The charismatic renewal spreads through those who are self-consciously identified with it, those who believe that others can have what they have received and offer it to them with the confidence that the Jesus who has 'baptised' and 'gifted' them wants to do the same for all his followers.

While the incidence varies enormously, we have seen enough to demonstrate continuity through the last two thousand years. Even if that has not been established, what cannot be denied is that charismatic phenomena are more widespread than ever at the beginning of the twenty-first century.

4

WHAT IS AN 'EVANGELICAL'?

Although a century older than 'charismatic', this label has also acquired a number of different meanings.

It is used of *some unbelievers*. From salesmen to politicians, those who are enthusiastic in selling goods or persuading others of the rightness of their opinions are said to do so with 'evangelical' fervour. This use is not unrelated to the activities of crusade evangelists. Nor is it irrelevant to the definition we shall be giving and employing.

It is used of *all believers*. Since the essential meaning of the word is 'gospel' (the Greek noun *euangelion* and verb *euangelizo* mean respectively 'good news' and 'announce good news'), it is claimed that all 'Christians' have in some way responded to the gospel, as they understand it.

Again, there is an element of truth in this wider application, but it is not used freely in all streams of church life. It is usually applied to one particular group, which may be found in most, if not all, denominations.

It is, then, used of *some believers*, to distinguish them from others. What is the difference?

As with 'charismatic', there is a popular understanding that focuses on behaviour. It is used to describe aggressive 'hot-gospellers' who are zealous in distributing tracts, buttonholing strangers and seeking to convert everybody they meet. It is also applied to evangelistic programmes, particularly those centred on famous evangelists.

But behind all behaviour lies certain beliefs and this is no exception. What, then, do 'evangelicals' believe? There are two elements, which provide our definition throughout this book.

THE CONTENT OF THE GOSPEL IS TO BE DEFENDED

Historically, the word emerged during the first half of the nineteenth century in reaction to Roman Catholic dogma which had infiltrated the Church of England through the Oxford Movement to form an Anglo-Catholic wing (one of its leaders, Newman, later transferred to Rome and became a Cardinal). There was a growing misgiving that doctrines and practices were being introduced that had no basis in scripture and, indeed, were contrary to its teaching. Tradition was being added to scripture and being given equal, if not superior, authority.

'Evangelicals' held to the Reformation principle of authority: scripture alone. They saw little difference between Roman additions to apostolic doctrine and those of cults and sects arising later that century and usually across the Atlantic (Joseph Smith and his *Book of Mormon*; Mary Baker Eddy and her *Science and Health*). Adding 'inspired' writing to the Bible was like piling luggage into a canoe; it would soon lose balance and overturn.

As the nineteenth gave way to the twentieth century, evangelicals found themselves fighting on another, opposite, front. From Germany came a 'liberal' attitude to the Bible called 'higher criticism', which applied Enlightenment philosophy, with its anti-supernaturalism, to the scriptures, many parts of which were no longer acceptable as they stood. Historical narratives were dismissed as myth, miracles as incredible and some statements about God as offensive. The whole was reinterpreted in evolutionary terms, as a development from crude and primitive ideas to refined and sophisticated understanding (i.e. that of the 'modern scholars'!).

This subtraction from scripture was seen by evangelicals as more dangerous than addition. The Bible minus was more corrosive than the Bible plus. 'Evangelical' became more antithetic to 'liberal' than to 'Catholic' (with some exceptions, particularly in Northern Ireland). The door had been opened to radical re-interpretation of the gospel – in psychological, sociological or even political categories.

At heart, then, evangelicals held to a high view of scripture, its divine inspiration and therefore its infallibility and its authority. They stood for the Bible, the whole Bible and nothing but the Bible.

Not that they always agreed on its interpretation, as distinct from its inspiration – nor have they always been careful enough to distinguish between the two! Some are more 'conservative' in their attitude to biblical scholarship, some more liberal. There have been deep differences in eschatology, particularly concerning the events preceding and succeeding the second coming of Christ.

What has united them is a common understanding of the gospel; they are of one mind as to what constitutes its 'fundamental' features (this was the original meaning of 'fundamentalist'; alas, it has now become a pejorative synonym for obscurantist or literalist).

They have therefore been prone to produce 'Statements of Faith' summarising these essential elements of the gospel. They usually include those beliefs about the Lord Jesus Christ questioned by liberal thinking: his virgin birth, his bodily resurrection and his personal return to earth. They also highlight those principles of salvation undermined by Catholic teaching, for example, justification by faith alone. Eschatological events are invariably included, particularly judgement, heaven and hell. In so far as God is defined, his wrath, justice and holiness will be put alongside his love and mercy.

Since all such statements (and the historic creeds of the church) reflect the contemporary controversies which elicited them, they need constant revision to meet new challenges. The situation in the last decade of the twentieth century radically changed. Liberalism was now much more radical and, since the second Vatican Council, has made huge inroads into the Roman Catholic church; at the same time a new movement called Evangelical Catholicism has produced a statement of beliefs which would astonish and delight many Protestants (significantly, it is also 'charismatic').

However, the apostolic gospel is, and will always be, the same. It needs to be translated into current thought-forms and words, but it must never be modified in the process. Evangelicals are unitedly concerned to 'contend for the faith that was once delivered to the saints' (Jude 3; one of their favourite texts). They empathise with Paul's aversion to, and anathema on, any 'other gospel' (Gal 1:9). That is because they are absolutely convinced that only one gospel is 'the power of God for the salvation of everyone who believes' (Rom 1:16). Nothing less is at stake than the salvage of the human race.

But the gospel will not save anyone by being preserved; it must be propagated as well to achieve its potential. The second 'evangelical' principle inevitably follows, and flows from, the first.

THE CONTENTS OF THE GOSPEL ARE
TO BE DECLARED

Those who believe they have found the cure, the only cure, for the ills of mankind can hardly keep it to themselves. As Paul said: 'Woe to me if I do not preach the gospel' (1 Cor 9:16).

Evangelicals take very seriously the 'Great Commission' of the departing Christ to 'go and make disciples of all nations' (Matt 28:19), to 'preach the gospel to every creature' (Mark 16:15), to 'preach repentance and forgiveness in his name' (Luke 24:47). They believe his return awaits the completion of the task of 'preaching the gospel of the kingdom in the whole world as a testimony to all nations' (Matt 24:14; note that 'nations' refers to ethnic groups, rather than political states).

They are also highly motivated by the eternal consequences of being 'lost' and are almost alone in still believing in the traditional understanding of hell (though this is now under debate; see my book *The Road to Hell*, reprinted by Terra Nova Publications, 2007).

More recently there has been a growing concern to apply the gospel to social action as well as in direct evangelism, though the latter is always held to be primary.

It is hardly surprising that this stream has produced such a large number of missionaries, perhaps the majority in the twentieth century. They have also counted among their ranks some of the best-known evangelists (Billy Graham and Luis Palau spring readily to mind).

In other words, evangelicals are both defensive and aggressive when it comes to the gospel. They are determined to preserve and propagate this message of hope for mankind which they have found in the Bible, which they believe to be both God's words and his Word, mediated through inspired human authors.

5

WHY HAVE EVANGELICALS NOT BEEN CHARISMATIC?

The discerning reader will already be asking this question. If the New Testament church was consistently charismatic (as shown in Chapter 2) and evangelicals appeal to scripture as their final authority (as stated in Chapter 4), why have they not been the same?

It is true that in recent years an increasing number of evangelicals have claimed to be 'charismatic' and many more have professed to be 'open' to that position. But the fact remains that for the greater part of their history they have been non-charismatic and even anti-charismatic. Many still are.

Why has the call back to scripture not led back to the Spirit, to the experience of the gift and the exercise of the gifts?

Some take refuge in the sovereignty of God and assume that he decides if and when the Holy Spirit acts in these ways.

It is not for us to know the times and seasons. We are not to desire or seek what he is not giving or doing.

But this is a subtle way of rejecting the life of the early church as normal, treating it as a time of 'revival'. Yet the New Testament writers were conscious of having entered a new era of the Spirit, the 'last days', which would not end until the 'day of the Lord' when all things would be restored.

There is clearly more to be said. It is legitimate to ask if human factors have been influencing history, before we attribute any characteristic feature to divine intention.

The truth is that, despite their appeal to scripture as their sole authority, evangelicals have been profoundly affected by tradition as well, though without always being fully conscious that this was happening. These traditions were Protestant rather than Catholic and therefore more recent. Both in principle and in practice, they left little or no room for the charismatic dimension. We shall consider three – Protestant reformation, Puritan preaching and dispensational theology.

PROTESTANT REFORMATION

The core of this sixteenth-century movement was the rediscovery of the Bible. Erasmus' publication of the New Testament in its original Greek, Luther's translations into German and Gutenberg's invention of printing all helped to make the scriptures accurately and widely known. Comparisons between what was found in its pages and what was taught by the priests was inevitable. Soon it was realised how much had been added to biblical piety – seven sacraments instead of two, purgatory and limbo as well as heaven and hell, prayers to Mary and the saints in addition to Father and Son, pilgrimages and the veneration of relics on top of prayer and fasting.

We owe a great deal to the courage of Luther and Melanchthon in Germany, Zwingli and Calvin in Switzerland. They realised that the simplicity of the early church had been so corrupted that the gospel itself had been changed, with tragic consequences. In particular, two fundamental principles had been compromised.

First, *justification by faith*. The net effect of all the additional duties was to introduce self-justification by works. Salvation could be earned by human effort, even bought with money. It was the sale of 'indulgences' (to reduce the time of the dead in purgatory), in aid of the building of St Peter's church in Rome, which sparked off the first 'protest' when Luther nailed his ninety-five 'theses' (debating points) to the church door in Wittenberg. The rediscovery of Paul's teaching about justification in his letter to the Romans may be said to be the key that unlocked all that followed.

Second, the *pre-eminence of Christ*. When Luther was asked by his superior, von Staupitz, what he would put in the place of prayers to saints, veneration of relics, devotion to Mary and pilgrimages to shrines, he replied: 'Christ. Man only needs Jesus Christ.' He and other Reformers realised that the introduction of other mediators, human and heavenly, had robbed Christ of his unique place in the life of the church and the individual member. The biblical concept of the priesthood of all believers restored his position.

This restoration of Christocentric faith and life was perhaps the greatest gain of the Reformation, which could be described as the rediscovery of the second person of the Trinity. Christianity is Christ – not an institution, not an ethic, not a culture, but a relationship based on trust and obedience with the Christ revealed in scripture.

So much was regained – but not all. The Reformers had their limitations. Those who idolise, or idealise, them tend to share those limits. They need to think beyond them, both back to the first century and forward to the twenty-first. The Reformation needs to be completed.

They rediscovered the second but not the third person of the Trinity. It is true that they frequently referred to him in *theological* ways (though it is alarming to find how few pages are devoted to the Spirit in Calvin's *Institutes of the Christian Religion*, compared to the huge section on the Ten Commandments). But there is a conspicuous absence of the 'experimental', or experiential, aspect. The two charismatic principles were never discussed.

One reason for this neglect may lie in the means used to establish Protestantism. Whole communities were changed by corporate legislation from above rather than by individual persuasion from below. The magistrates enforced the change (hence the title: 'Magisterial Reformers').

Those who sought to free the church and state from each other, seeing the church as a voluntary fellowship of individual believers (admitted by adult baptism), were only seeking to carry the process of reformation to its logical conclusion but were rejected as traitors by Protestant and Catholic alike. Significantly, it was in this 'left-wing' group ('Anabaptists', 'Spiritists') that charismatic features reappeared. However, their enforced separation from the main stream made them vulnerable to imbalance and excess.

Another feature of the 'right-wing' which may have a bearing on our survey, was an excessive emphasis on predestination. Luther was even more Calvinist than Calvin in this respect! Both were following Augustine. This has tended to encourage a passive waiting for the Spirit rather than an active seeking, as well as implying that his power is for those who are chosen to receive it, rather than for every believer. (Later pentecostalism sprang from Arminian roots, with an emphasis on human responsibility and co-operation with the divine initiative.)

We must also note that the Reformers faced widespread superstition within the church, particularly in connection with shrines and relics. The people had no problem believing in miracles, especially healing; indeed, they were too gullible in such matters, directing their faith towards objects and actions rather than the Lord Jesus. In rightly stamping out such abuses, the Reformers may well have failed to distinguish between spurious superstition and genuine supernaturalism, throwing out the baby with the bath water. Certainly, they showed no inclination to reconsider healing and other miracles as biblical fact rather than medieval fantasy.

In summary, evangelicals of the Reformed tradition have had considerable difficulty in assimilating charismatic convictions into their theological system, but a number are now attempting to do so.

PURITAN PREACHING

The Reformation replaced the medieval dispensing of the (seven) sacraments with the ministry of word and (two) sacraments, of which the former soon took prior place. It was still limited to those who were ordained, though this had lost its sacerdotal (priestly) implications and therefore, at least in theory, its monopoly.

Worship soon centred on, and led up to, the sermon. Preaching probably reached its peak during the Puritan era. The very architecture of church buildings erected at that time is revealing. The dimension and location of the pulpit provided optimum sight and sound for the preacher. The people are arranged in straight rows to 'sit under the Word'. These 'preaching-houses' are built to contain one gift of one man. Apart from joining in the praise and prayer (often silently with the latter), the 'congregation' are not expected to exercise gifts or ministries, which belong to the pulpit (or platform) rather than the pew.

This allowed no room for what has come to be called 'body ministry', in which any member can minister to the others. Though clearly the pattern of meetings in the early church (1 Cor 14:26), it was never even considered as a possibility, much less a necessity. Ministry was the province of '*the* minister'.

The emphasis was on exposition rather than experience. Powerful and persuasive preaching was sometimes identified with New Testament 'prophesying', though in this respect the problem of Paul's permitting women to prophesy but not to teach was never resolved (1 Cor 11:5; 1 Tim 2:12).

It was not so much that the Puritans were opposed to things charismatic in principle; it was more that in practice there was simply no provision for them, perhaps indicating a lack of interest, due in turn to a lack of personal experience.

Evangelicals who revere and emulate the Puritans are apt to assume that their ignoring, even ignorance of, these issues proves their irrelevance. If they got on so well without them, why can't we?

DISPENSATIONAL THEOLOGY

When J.N. Darby and his colleagues founded the 'Brethren' in Dublin, they consciously sought to return to the 'free' worship of the early church, allowing the Spirit to lead with contributions from anyone present. Within a short time, spiritual gifts began to appear, notably tongues and prophecy. A conference was held to consider this unexpected development. Because they were already strongly suspect in orthodox circles, it was felt that such controversial innovations could cause irreparable damage to the infant movement and a decision to discourage them was reluctantly taken. Certainly tongues were already a subject of fierce debate because of the Irvingites, with whom Darby had links through Dr Drummond of Albury.

As the Brethren developed their doctrine, largely through the writings of Darby, they adopted a 'dispensational' interpretation of the Bible. The history of mankind was divided into distinct periods or 'dispensations' (usually seven), in each of which God deals with man on a different basis. Another feature was the complete separation of future destinies for Jew and Gentile, Israel and the church.

One of these 'dispensations' was the age of grace or the age of the church, which covers the centuries between the first and second advents of Christ. But once having started dividing time up in this way, it was difficult to stop and an implicit division of this age into apostolic and post-apostolic eras followed. The more unusual activities of the Spirit were limited to the former. The spiritual gifts (*charismata*) were not to be expected, much less encouraged, subsequently.

Dispensational thinking was taken across the Atlantic by Darby and embraced by Dr Scofield, who incorporated it in his annotated Bible. Through seminaries like Dallas and popular authors like Hal Lindsay, this viewpoint has had a very profound influence on the evangelical scene. It seems to carry with it an inherent anti-charismatic emphasis.

Asserting that the special gifts are not for today, some explanation is required for their apparent reappearance in the twentieth century. At first, they were explained as satanic counterfeit, deceiving the elect. It was frequently said that:

'Tongues are of the devil', which could come dangerously close to the unforgivable sin (Matt 12:24, 32). More recently, they have been attributed to the flesh rather than the devil and tongues have even been diagnosed as harmless psychological activity!

Surprisingly, pentecostals, whose origins are largely American, have adopted much of the dispensational teaching and combined it with charismatic principles, though the latter sprang from a very different source, the Wesleyan Holiness stream. But in the main, 'dispensationalists' remain highly suspicious of this combination and, indeed, hostile to all charismatic claims.

* * * * *

Since the influence of Reformation, Puritan and dispensational viewpoints have been so widespread among evangelicals, though not usually together, it is understandable that they have overlooked the charismatic dimension of the gospel. And there is a further reason for their doing so.

Evangelicals have tended to use the epistles as their primary source of doctrine, rather than the gospels or Acts. In this, they may also have been influenced by the Reformers, who had the same priority. The book of Acts is classified as 'narrative' and therefore not directly appropriate for 'didactic' – teaching – use.

This is in spite of the following facts: that Acts and many epistles deal with the same places and people, that the epistles contain 'narrative' and Acts 'didactic' material, and that they often illuminate each other (for example, there is no way of understanding 'baptised in one Spirit' or 'receive Holy Spirit' in the epistles except by referring to Acts).

Furthermore, among the epistles the one written by Paul to the Romans is taken by evangelicals as a kind of yardstick by which to judge the others. It is assumed that it contains a complete summary of the gospel and that its omission of any explicit reference to baptism in, or gifts of, the Holy Spirit indicates their relative unimportance, even irrelevance.

Whether Paul ever intended his letter to be taken in this way may be questioned (Appendix A presents a very different understanding, which relates it, like all his others, to the situation and needs of his readers). But the real weakness is that it is creating a 'canon within a canon'. To take *part* of the New Testament, using that to construct a theological system into which all other parts must fit, is not the way to establish biblical theology. Data must be assembled from the *whole* (gospels, Acts, epistles and Revelation) before a comprehensive picture of the 'good news' of redemption can be obtained.

And we need to remember that all the letters were written to those who had *already* been initiated into the life in the Spirit. They had already 'received the Spirit' (Gal 3:2), been 'baptised in one Spirit' (1 Cor 12:13), had the Spirit 'poured out' upon them (Tit 3:5). This could be taken for granted and did not need to be explained, or even included. The fact that Paul wrote about spiritual gifts to the Corinthians was only occasioned by their abuse of them; otherwise we might not even have heard about them!

It is in Acts that we find out Paul's counsel to the unbeliever, the seeker, the enquirer. And there we learn of his concern that his converts 'receive' the Spirit, in addition to repenting of sin, believing in Jesus and being baptised in water – a concern he shared with Peter and John (Acts 8:14–17; 19:1–7).

Even in Romans we sense his desire to 'impart some spiritual gift' to them for their strengthening (Rom 1:14). Though this is more explicit in other letters (e.g. his wish that all spoke in tongues as he did; 1 Cor 14:5, 18), that does not reduce the value of his comments. Yet this aspect has been largely ignored.

As has been demonstrated in this chapter, there are human reasons for the failure of evangelicals to incorporate charismatic insights into their understanding of the gospel.

However, this traditional 'blindspot' (and don't we all have them?) has been seriously challenged by the massive re-emergence of 'pentecostal' phenomena in the twentieth century. How have they coped with this development, so alien to their principles and practice?

6

HOW HAVE EVANGELICALS RELATED TO CHARISMATICS?

Up to 1900, they could virtually ignore them, for there were so few by comparison. This attitude is no longer possible. The twentieth century witnessed a dramatic change in the ratio. Charismatic numbers have rapidly caught up with evangelicals and look like overtaking them in the twenty-first century.

The first half of the twentieth-century development focused on emerging pentecostal denominations, so that charismatic expression was segregated from traditional churches. But the second half saw an unexpected emergence of similar phenomena within the mainline denominations, together with a minor explosion of new fellowships, independent or networked (often referred to as 'house' churches, where they usually first met).

One complication, which has puzzled, embarrassed and sometimes irritated evangelicals is that most, though not all, charismatics are also evangelical – whereas the reverse has not been the case. This has also made it difficult to ignore, much less disown, them.

It is possible to discern four phases in the relationship, at least as far as the majority of evangelicals is concerned (all four attitudes can still be found today). There is both change and development.

We shall call these phases 'waves', partly because the 'third' has already been given this title and has entered common usage.

Of course, any such analysis is open to the charge of over-simplification; but that can assist understanding. Caricature can aid recognition, provided its limitations are accepted.

FIRST WAVE – SUSPICION

When the first 'pentecostal' activity broke out at the turn of the twentieth century, both in America and this country, it was far from welcome. Indeed, it was quite quickly rejected and not just in evangelical circles. This inevitably led to separate churches and denominations, which were at best isolated and at worst persecuted.

Though adherents apparently preached the same basic gospel, there was considerable suspicion of their orthodoxy over two doctrinal matters, which proved real 'sticking-points' to other evangelicals.

First, baptism in (or 'of') the Spirit was taught as a 'second blessing', distinct from conversion or regeneration (we shall be considering this phrase and its implications in a later chapter). This kind of language had been known (for example, in 'Wesleyan Holiness' teaching), though it had never been widespread. It became doubly offensive when linked to tongues.

Second, tongues were *the* evidence of this 'baptism' and released other 'gifts' in their wake. That this was a major offence is seen in the common evangelical description of what was happening: 'the tongues movement'.

An impartial observer of the conflict might also have suspected sociological factors. While evangelicals had made most headway among the middle and upper classes, 'pentecostals' seemed to be most effective at the lower end of the scale – among the socially handicapped, the ethnic minorities, the uneducated, the unskilled. Our 'observer' might have remarked on the fact that this was not dissimilar to the New Testament church (1 Cor 1:26–29)!

With this trend came a whole new style of worship, even less acceptable than the new teaching. Noisy rather than quiet, uninhibited rather than restrained, spontaneous rather than prepared – such meetings hardly conformed to the dignity of religious respectability.

So they were left alone to express themselves as they wished (in private, of course), in the hope that they would prove to be a passing fashion or at the most an eccentric minority. They were neither expected nor invited to meet with other Christian bodies.

But they grew.

SECOND WAVE – TOLERATION

Two developments made a new relationship possible.

On the one hand, 'pentecostals' became more acceptable and therefore more accepted. Early excesses and eccentricities died down. Their church buildings had been around long enough to be part of the scene. Their pastors were more educated (some even wore dog-collars!). National headquarters, organisations and colleges followed. In thus conforming to the existing denominational image, the way was open to become part of the church spectrum, if only at one extreme end of it.

On the other hand, 'pentecostalism' was penetrating the other denominations by the sixties. Though some 'classic' pentecostals (as the earlier ones were now called) were involved in this 'neopentecostal' movement (as it was called in the beginning), these links were soon down-played and 'charismatic renewal' became the new description.

Tolerance was now exhibited in two ways. Both old pentecostals and new charismatics were welcomed into larger enterprises, particularly united evangelistic crusades – though there was an unspoken understanding that they did not introduce their distinctive emphases on such occasions! Bodies like the Evangelical Alliance were thrown open, without any discrimination, while hesitant to acknowledge the contribution they could give.

At the level of the local church there was an increasing tolerance towards the exercise of gifts, though these were accepted rather than encouraged and not always allowed in Sunday services. Many clergy and ministers professed to be 'open' to such things (not a few having had a personal but private taste of them); but they were not convinced enough to preach positively about them or introduce others to them.

But a climate had been created in which discussion was possible and closer relations could be explored.

THIRD WAVE – COALITION

During the eighties, there was an open and sincere attempt to establish a mutual confidence that would move the situation beyond *détente*. Originating in America, associated with names like John Wimber and Peter Wagner, the venture soon crossed the Atlantic, with its chosen name: 'third wave'.

The prime aim was pragmatic – to bring evangelical and charismatic streams together in practice, for the evangelising and edifying ministry of the churches. There was little attempt to face any theological tensions. The philosophy seemed to be: 'The job needs us both; let's forget our differences and get on with it together.'

Such an approach has obvious appeal and strikes a chord with many. Yet it cannot be the last word. Theological issues cannot be swept aside so easily and have a habit of merely being postponed if they are not resolved. For real unity requires shared convictions as well as common objectives. Nor can any Christian project free itself from theological issues. 'Third wave' is no exception.

In two ways, a radical change had already been made in the charismatic position, whether consciously or unconsciously. Each represented a compromise and a concession.

First, the biblical locus of thinking had been shifted from Acts to the gospels, especially the three called 'Synoptic'

(Matthew, Mark and Luke). The ministry of Jesus and his disciples during those three years became the model or 'paradigm' of charismatic action. Attention was focused on healing and exorcism, rather than tongues. It was hardly noticed that this was to apply 'pre-Pentecost' standards. Yet this shift was to lead to an even more significant change.

Second, one of the two charismatic principles had now been dropped. Exercise of the gifts could now be stimulated without mentioning an experience of the gift. Such phraseology as 'baptised in Holy Spirit' could and should be dropped. It is not really needed. After all, the disciples were healing the sick and casting out demons before the day of Pentecost (this point was implicit, though it was not usually made explicit). All Christians can use the gifts without needing any special enduement with power.

What all this boils down to is an assurance that evangelicals can embrace charismatic gifts without any theological adjustment. But it is also an admission that charismatics have been profoundly mistaken in their understanding, not only of the significance of Pentecost but also in their conviction that Jesus is the one who baptises in Holy Spirit as well as being the Lamb of God who takes away the sin of the world (John 1:29, 33).

Reluctance to use biblical terminology can indicate an unwillingness to accept biblical theology. In this case, the doctrine of initiation is at stake. What is the apostolic answer to the question: how and when is the Holy Spirit 'received'?

It remains to be seen whether the exercise of gifts will be more or less frequent as a result of this concession. The long-term effects may indicate that this price for unity has been too high. There could well be a gradual decline of the charismatic dimension, if this approach is widely adopted.

But there is another possible way forward.

FOURTH WAVE – INTEGRATION

This begins with the fact that the New Testament is both evangelical and charismatic – in one stream, not two – that these were united at every level, especially in terms of theological conviction.

The 'fourth wave' will recover this unity, for the first time since the days of the apostles. No longer will terms like 'born-again Christians', 'Bible-believing Christians' or 'Spirit-filled Christians' be used, for they will be one and the same. 'Charismatic' and 'evangelical' will drop out of use, since each will include the other. Perhaps even 'Christian' will disappear; it was only a nickname coined and used by unbelievers – the believers preferred to call themselves 'disciples' or 'brothers'.

Every 'disciple' will have repented toward God, believed in Jesus and received (been baptised in, filled with) the Holy Spirit. Each disciple will have been given a 'grace-gift' with which to edify the church and evangelise the world.

All disciples will together be led by the Spirit in the light of scripture, developing his fruit as well as demonstrating the gifts.

If the early church, with all its faults, could be totally charismatic and totally evangelical, why can we not be the same? There must be a way of bringing these two aspects together. It can be done without compromise or concession; but it cannot be done without correction and confession.

It is obvious that if there are still differences it is because either or – more likely – both, have departed in some way from the original harmony. In other words, the way ahead is not one of compromise, but one of correction.

This involves a willingness to expose cherished concepts to ruthless comparison with the biblical data. It involves repentance in its basic sense of rethinking, seeking truth and reality (the two English words are the same in Hebrew and Greek).

Such an exercise calls for honesty on the part of both streams – in openly facing the real differences between them and, even more important, in considering whether there could be differences between these contradictory convictions and the apostolic doctrine revealed in the whole New Testament.

Since it is always easier to learn new truth than unlearn old tradition, there will be pain; but it will be creative – and redemptive.

When there are clear differences, both cannot be right; both could be wrong. But there can be no progress if each is absolutely sure that the other is the one that must be wrong.

Part II of this book seeks to suggest an agenda for such an exercise. Seven areas are presented, in each of which self-correction could provide a breakthrough. Both streams are invited to reconsider their position on each issue.

The intended objective is convergence rather than controversy, not by trying to find some point of balance or middle ground between the two, but by calling both from the present dialectic to a true synthesis based on scripture.

The good news is that this 'fourth wave' is already here, but largely at a personal level. It is against human nature to live with contradictions and many evangelicals coming into a charismatic experience have had to wrestle with the questions this has raised. Heart and mind have to be in harmony; we need to think and feel right about what we say and do.

Of course, many have shrunk from the adventure, fearful of the risks involved, unwilling to endanger their mental security. They have simply not tried to integrate their new experience with their old theology. They have hung on to all their former doctrines, whether they were Roman or Reformed, Calvinist or Arminian, evangelical or pentecostal.

But a growing number are willing to let the Spirit guide them into all truth, believing that 'the Lord has yet more light to bring forth from his word' (as one of the Pilgrim Fathers put it). Such are invited to come into the second half of this book with an open mind and an obedient will.

We shall be exploring the place of theology, the nature of

scripture, the doctrine of initiation, the gift of tongues, the extent of ministry and the way of holiness. But we shall only consider those facets of each which are relevant to our purpose of bringing evangelical and charismatic into agreement and unity.

Note

I coined the phrase 'Fourth Wave' to describe what I hoped would happen next, but was only then seen on a local and limited scale. The rest of the book described the necessary integration to make it as general as the three preceding 'waves'. Since publication, the term has been used of the 'Toronto blessing' and subsequent related events. This was not what I had in mind, so the title has been changed to avoid confusion. However, it is retained here as a sub-heading since I am still convinced it is what the Lord wanted as the final stage of the twentieth century renewal of his church.

J. D. P. 1998

PART II

THE DIFFERENCES RESOLVED

7

THEOLOGY

Theology may be simply defined as thinking about God, using our reason to understand him better, loving him with all our mind.

All rational processes begin with presuppositions. Assumptions provide the starting-point. In the case of biblical theology, God's self-revelation in scripture is taken for granted as the data from which doctrine is to be constructed.

Every Christian, indeed every person, has a theology. Everyone has their own ideas about 'God', even agnostics (that he is unknowable) and atheists (that he doesn't exist). Christians believe that all claims to knowledge of God, including their own, must be tested against the standard ('canon') of scripture, taken as a whole. So the first question of any theology is: how true to the Bible is it?

Then comes a very practical second question: how far is that theology influencing the life and affecting the behaviour of those who hold it? It is possible for theology to play too small a role (a charismatic trend!) or too large a role (an evangelical trend!). Relating theology and experience is a delicate operation and imbalance is a constant risk.

EXPERIENCE IS NOT THEOLOGY

We are living through an 'existential' era. It is a time of subjective sensations with a stress, a reliance, on feelings. The search for emotional stimulation takes many forms —chemical, sexual, musical and spiritual. The test of reality is whether it feels good.

Subjectivism is always introverted, self-centred. The eighties were labelled 'the *me* decade', with their characteristic emphasis on self-expression, self-fulfilment, self-esteem and self-love. Sometimes called 'the youth culture', it was by no means limited to that section of the age range.

At the same time there was a parallel change inside the churches. The introduction of electronically amplified music led to a style of worship that at times resembled a disco or an aerobics class. Books and sermons exhorted believers to love themselves as they loved their neighbours, to 'let it all hang out' in worship and to discover their potential gifts. Many sought to be baptised in the Spirit, though it was possible they were seeking an experience to satisfy as much as equipment to serve.

What was to be made of all this? Was it a move of God or not? Three opinions emerged.

Some said it was all *human conformity*. They could see little difference between the 'flower people' and the 'Jesus movement'. It was yet another case of the world getting into the church, this time on a massive scale. Those who made this diagnosis were led, of course, to an attitude of total rejection of all these 'new' things, which were often lumped together under the label 'charismatic'.

Others said it was the *divine counterpoint*. God was meeting the new generation at the point of their need, providing the answer to their search with an authentic spiritual experience to replace the many spurious substitutes. Better to be filled with the Spirit and 'get high on Jesus' than stupefied by drugs and alcohol (Ephesians 5:18 provides a precedent for this kind of thinking!). The result of this diagnosis was total acceptance of all that was happening. If it brought people in, it was welcomed. If it 'worked', it was OK.

A few realised that it could be a *mixture of both*, of world and church, flesh and Spirit. Total rejection and total acceptance were both inappropriate responses. The situation cried out for discernment and discrimination. Yet the mood was not sympathetic to critical appraisal and few would have known how to set about it.

The fact is that there are three possible sources of all

spiritual experiences – God, ourselves and the devil (it is a false dichotomy to say that what is not of God must be of the devil). For every divine gift there is a fleshly substitute and a demonic counterfeit. There are three categories of speaking in tongues; the same is true of faith healing. There is a healthy fear of deception that falls short of a paralysing phobia. Cautious exploration is better than habitual hesitation.

How can we distinguish between true and false experiences? One way is to wait for the ultimate fruits, in terms of the effect on the relationship with the Lord and the outworking of that in daily living. But by the time such evidence appears, it is often too late. We need more immediate tests.

One of the most important spiritual gifts is the 'ability to distinguish between spirits' (1 Cor 12:10). Its possessor knows by inspired intuition the source from which a spiritual phenomenon springs. What a useful gift and what a safeguard! Yet it is rarely sought and even more rarely exercised. That is because it demands confrontation, which is not well received and requires considerable maturity and courage.

This gift (of discernment) is only given to some, yet we are all exhorted to 'test all things' (1 Thess 5:22f). There is one test we can all apply: what does the Bible say about it?

It has to be admitted that charismatics have not always been eager to apply this test. They have sometimes forgotten that the actions of the Spirit will always agree with the revelations of scripture, since the latter was the result of the former. The

Holy Spirit, like the other two persons of the Trinity, is totally consistent in character and conduct.

The result has been that theology has sometimes been built on experience rather than vice-versa. There has been a noticeable streak of pragmatism in charismatic thinking: 'if we felt led to do it and it worked, it must be of the Spirit.' Since it is helpful (though not always welcome!) to be specific, we give two examples. In both cases, the use of unbiblical terminology is significant.

There is a charismatic experience known as 'being slain in the Spirit'. It is an extraordinary phrase. I was once asked, in a pastors' seminar, what I thought about it. I assured them it had biblical precedent – Ananias and Sapphira both had the experience, after lying about how much they put in the offertory! Of course, they saw I had neatly evaded the question, though I was trying to teach them to be more careful about language (the milder version, 'resting in the Spirit', is no more biblical). So they changed the wording of the question to 'falling on the ground'. I assured them that this also could be found in scripture and had happened to Ezekiel, Paul, John and others. But in no case were they 'pushed' over by the Spirit; in every case it was a human reaction rather than a divine action, much less an 'evidence' of the latter. Indeed, those who collapsed were often told to stand up again and on one occasion it was the Spirit who raised them up. So there is more biblical warrant for being picked up (Ezek 2:1f) than pushed over by the Spirit!

That it happened then and still happens now is indisputable as a matter of experience; it was acceptable by the inspired authors of scripture and should be by us. But when a theological interpretation is put upon it, without biblical warrant, the result is confusion and even bondage. When people being ministered to in prayer collapse, it is taken as 'proof' that the work has been done and ministry can be concluded, whereas this may not be the case at all (it can even be an evasion of further help, especially in the case of the 'demonised'). Worse still, the success of a meeting, or even the man leading it, may be assessed by the number of those 'hitting the deck'! Those who have not gone 'weak at the knees' can be left with self-doubts about their faith or reception of divine help. I was even once asked by a nun to pray that she would fall down, since she had never had the experience!

Such distortions and abuses would never have occurred had the phenomenon been checked out with the Bible from the beginning. It would neither have been rejected nor encouraged, but simply accepted as a natural response to becoming the focus of divine attention. It would be described in biblical terms as 'falling down'.

Another example, with wider implications, is the charismatic doctrine of 'spiritual warfare', with particular reference to 'territorial spirits'. This encourages those engaging in mission, both evangelism and social action, to identify the demonic powers controlling the proposed location and wrestle in prayer until they are 'bound' in the name of Jesus, thus releasing the area before engaging in more practical activity.

This approach began with the experience of a project attempted by 'Youth with a Mission' which made no progress until this was done. Success attended its repetition. There is now a whole body of teaching on the subject, both verbal and printed. Though scriptures are now claimed to support the method, its origins did not lie in a rediscovery of the biblical nature of mission.

When examined in the light of scripture, the evidence is meagre, to say the least. Certainly, the world is clearly populated with demonic agents, not least because the devil is not omnipresent; he can only be in one place at once (Job 1:7; Luke 4:13). Certainly, Jesus had to 'bind' the strong man before he could spoil his goods (Matt 12:29). Certainly, he and his disciples engaged in exorcism, confronting and casting demons out of individuals (Matt 10:7). Certainly, this ministry was expected to be continued by later believers (Mark 16:17). Having said all this, there are limits to its application.

There are only two verses in the whole Bible that explicitly describe 'territorial' spirits (Dan 9:13, 20). Even then, it is not entirely clear whether the 'princes' of Persia and Greece are human or demonic, though most scholars assume the latter. What needs to be noted is that Daniel did not directly engage them, nor was he commanded to do so. They were dealt with by angelic intervention.

One striking feature of engagement with demons by Jesus and others in the New Testament is that they never took the initiative. They never went looking for them. Only when demons manifested themselves were they confronted and banished and even then not always immediately, as if their interference was a distraction (Acts 16:18).

There is certainly no trace of starting missions in any new place by binding the local demonic ruler, no hint that Paul sought to identify and bind the spirits of Athens or Corinth before preaching there. Were this an essential prerequisite for releasing a situation, it would surely have been specifically included in the ascending Lord's missionary mandate (e.g. Matt 28:18–20). There is no apostolic precedent, either in precept or practice. Neither is there any command for believers to 'bind' the devil.

There is, however, considerable precedent for testing claimed activity of the Spirit by an appeal to scripture. The outstanding example is to be found in the council at Jerusalem (Acts 15). Paul had challenged the apostles and elders of the church over the matter of circumcision. Peter reported the charismatic experience of the uncircumcised. James demonstrated its compatibility with scriptural statement. And everybody was satisfied with the final conclusion, expressed by the one who brought the biblical contribution. Would that all our controversies were handled so well!

Charismatics, then, must be willing to have their teaching examined from this perspective, willing to concede that some of it has very slender grounds in scripture and cannot be insisted upon as part of Christian truth.

Without an openness to evangelical questioning, they expose themselves to the danger of uncritical acceptance of special revelations, which could make them vulnerable to heresy and immorality. In the history of the church there are a number of examples of this happening to 'charismatic' groups, the Montanists being one.

There are positive values in exposing experience to biblical theology. Note at least three reasons for doing so.

First, to *test* what is happening. Those who believe in a God of truth with a passion for reality should be the first to want to separate the genuine from the spurious. They will not rest content with anything less than the real thing. They will fear deceiving themselves and others. They will hate hypocrisy. Spiritual claims that cannot or will not be tested by scripture would be approached with extreme caution.

Second, to *understand* what is happening. The whole of scripture is event plus interpretation. What God does is accompanied by an explanation as to why he does it. Fear of supernatural events can be due to fear of the unknown. Switching on the light cures fear of darkness. Fear of being 'taken over' by the Spirit is removed by the scriptural teaching that his fruit is self-control and the gifts are subject to the will of those who use them (Gal 5:23; 1 Cor 14:32).

Third, to *communicate* what is happening. Feelings are personal to each individual and impossible to pass on to others. Attempts to do so slide into the dangerous practice of manipulation (not unknown in Christian circles). Emotionalism is the result, with feelings stimulated from the outside rather than welling up from the inside.

But biblical experience can be communicated, not by attempts to reproduce it, but by passing on the spiritual truths from which it springs. The process is therefore indirect – from one human spirit to another by the means of scripture, all in the power of the Holy Spirit. To by-pass the objective revelation is to encourage subjective relativism (what feels real to me is true for me).

To be real, religious experience must be experienced theology. Equally, if theology is to be real, it must be experienced, as we shall now see.

DOCTRINE IS NOT DYNAMIC

It is not entirely unknown for evangelicals to build their theology on experience – particularly on their 'bad' experience of encountering eccentric charismatics! But their more usual weakness is to divorce theology from experience.

It has been said that where Catholics worshipped the Trinity of Father, Son and Virgin Mary, Protestants substituted Father, Son and holy scripture. The jibe has truth in it – for both parties.

It is sadly true that some, perhaps many, evangelicals know

the Bible better than they know the Spirit – or, at least, that they are more conscious of their relationship to the book than the person. This comes out in conversation and discussion, when it is more 'natural' to refer to the wording of scripture than the leading of the Spirit.

In some circles, believers are described as 'sound' if they know the right texts, give the right answers and hold the right views. Faith becomes an intellectual acceptance of the Bible, a mental assent to its doctrines. It is treated as a collection of proof-texts. Teaching scripture is primarily a matter of looking up references. It is assumed that to know the Bible is to know the Lord.

This approach invariably involves separation from those who are not considered 'sound' in doctrine. This tendency to divide is sometimes extended to the point of isolating those who may be orthodox themselves but who relate with those who are not, a practice known as 'guilt by association'. The result is that circles of fellowship become progressively smaller and more exclusive.

Here, then, are two issues: the relationship of doctrine to life and the relationship of doctrine to fellowship. We will take them in that order.

Evangelicals are shocked when reminded that God neither inspired nor intended his word to be divided up by chapter and verse numbers. For the first thousand years, Christians lacked such conveniences. They really knew their Bibles then – by context rather than text.

And the context is always a life-situation. The Bible is neither a collection of texts nor a treatise on systematic theology (wouldn't it be convenient if each book concentrated on one doctrine?). It is the living word of the living God to living people – to be lived out.

Doctrine is to be done (the little word 'do' is one of the most common in Old and New Testaments and is the heart of Jesus' shortest parable: Matt 21:28–32). It was Jesus who said that whoever chooses to do the will of God will know the doctrine (John 7:17). Justification by faith alone was never meant to be mental assent alone. As Calvin said, 'faith is never alone'. James, the Lord's brother, made it quite clear that faith without actions is dead and 'cannot save' (Jas 2:14–26).

Theology is more than logic. It is life. This is particularly true in relation to the Holy Spirit. Doctrine is not dynamic. It is possible to have an impeccable understanding of his person and work while remaining impotent in the face of need or evil.

Scripture does not exhort us to 'believe in' the Spirit, but to 'receive' him. When Paul asked the Ephesian disciples whether (or when) they had 'received Holy Spirit', he was checking on their experience rather than their doctrine. The apostles would have been astonished at the modern notion that he is received 'by faith' – that is, you convince yourself that he has been given even when absolutely nothing has happened. We repeat an earlier point that, if this were the case in the New Testament, nobody could possibly have known that the Samaritans had not received the Spirit (Acts 8:16) – or when they did!

We are to communicate the gospel by demonstration as well as declaration (Mark 16:20; Luke 10:9; Rom 15:18f; 1 Cor 2:4; 1 Thess 1:5). People need to see as well as hear (Matt 13:16f; John 11:45; Acts 2:33; Heb 2:4; Jas 2:18). This requires more than sound doctrine. An understanding of the person of the Spirit must be matched by an anointing with his power. We may deliver an excellent lecture *about* him but that may not develop an experienced life *in* him.

The fact is that, while there has been some talk about the Holy Spirit in evangelical circles, this has not led many to experience the gift or exercise the gifts. However, this is not due just to an overemphasis on 'believing' and an under-emphasis on living. As we shall see (in Chapter 9), the doctrine that was taught and accepted in evangelical circles was defective at one or two crucial points (notably in the confusing invitation to 'receive' Jesus).

Turning to the second question of the relationship of doctrine to fellowship, we face a major obstacle to improving relations. The problem is an extreme reluctance in non-charismatic evangelicals to consider meeting with non-evangelical charismatics. The latter are gathered at the opposite end of the ecclesiastical spectrum, comprising some Anglo-Catholics and many, many Roman Catholics.

Evangelicals with a Reformed tradition find it virtually impossible to believe that a genuine move of the Spirit could be taking place among those who still embrace dogmas and duties which they consider to be so contrary to scripture. As explained above, their revulsion can be extended to fellow evangelicals who accept it as genuine, even regarding them as traitors.

It must be freely admitted that many charismatics, with their weakness for exalting experience over theology, have been guilty of doctrinal indifference. Revelling in the joy of worship and fellowship with a whole new crowd, they have often forgotten, or at least ignored, the real and important differences between them. This has led to compromise. Love has been emphasised at the expense of truth. A united front has been presented in public which could not be sustained in private if differences were honestly faced.

Given all this, there is still one vital question for evangelicals: is doctrine the starting-point for Christian fellowship? Should I extend a hand only to those who share my theological position (which implies that I am totally orthodox) or to all those to whom my Lord has given his Spirit (even though they still hold what I would consider heterodox or even heretical views)?

Does scripture help us with this dilemma? Two strands of apostolic teaching come to mind, one qualifying the other.

On the one hand, we are encouraged to accept those whom God has accepted and to whom he has given his Spirit. They are brothers and sisters with the same Father. And we are not to expect of them more than we hope they expect of us. There will be babies as well as adults in every family. Believers will not be immediately perfect, either in belief or behaviour. They are to be loved, nurtured, encouraged and corrected until they are mature.

Two epistles of Paul illustrate this. He addressed the Corinthians as 'brethren', in spite of apparent disbelief in the resurrection among them, to say nothing of immorality (a point we shall take up in Chapter 12). They needed correction in belief and behaviour, yet Paul did not ostracise them (some ecclesiastical authorities today might disown a church condoning incest in its membership and intoxication at communion services!). He recognised them as babies, as 'carnal' rather than 'spiritual'. They had all been 'baptised in Spirit' and had all the 'spiritual gifts' (1 Cor 1:7; 12:13).

Writing to the Ephesians, Paul exhorts them to 'make every effort to keep the unity of the Spirit through the bond of peace' (Eph 4:3). This acknowledges that they are already 'one body' through 'having shared one Spirit' (v. 4). He goes on to describe the gifts of ministry distributed in the church by the ascended Lord 'to prepare God's people for works of service, so that the body of Christ may be built up' (v. 12). Then come the crucial words: '*until we all reach unity in the faith* and in the knowledge of the son of God and become mature, attaining to the whole measure of the fulness of Christ' (v. 13). So we are to maintain the unity of the Spirit until we reach unity in the faith. Doctrinal agreement is the goal, not the basis, of unity. We start with the fellowship (*koinonia*) of the Spirit and on that foundation build a mature understanding of faith in and knowledge of our common Lord.

But this needs to be qualified by the many warnings in scripture against false prophets and teachers with their deceptive perversions of the gospel. Truth and love belong together (Eph 4:15). Believers need to 'contend for the faith that was once entrusted to the saints' (Jude 3). Anyone twisting the gospel is to be cursed (Gal 1:9); they must not even be given hospitality (2 John 7–11). The church is more easily damaged by internal perversion than external persecution.

The solution to this tension lies in drawing a firm distinction between fellowship and ministry. It is a delicate balance, requiring spiritual sensitivity. It will involve accepting some as fellow-believers but not accepting them as teachers. This discrimination will need to be lovingly explained or it will be quickly misunderstood.

Unless such a distinction is made, we shall remain stuck in the present impasse — charismatics accepting ministry from all with whom they enjoy fellowship and evangelicals refusing fellowship with all from whom they could not accept ministry. Both streams need more discernment and wisdom in handling this situation.

If charismatics need to be more firm in upholding the truth, evangelicals need to be more flexible in expressing love. To exalt truth at the expense of love is as questionable as exalting love at the expense of truth. Speaking the truth in love is the way to unity, since, as we have already said, real unity depends on shared convictions.

Perhaps the most delicate question is whether our initial unity in the Spirit should be publicly displayed before reaching a measure of unity in the faith; for example, by speaking from the same platform. This has probably been the greatest stumbling block for evangelicals in charismatic behaviour. Their hesitation is understandable and, in some cases, commendable, since such situations are a mixture of fellowship and ministry. Yet they must recognise that each situation is unique and must be considered on its merits. And they must believe that some charismatics have not been without prayerful, even painful, heart-searching before engaging in such occasions.

The tensions are unlikely to be resolved until all evangelicals are charismatic and all charismatics are evangelical. Which happens first depends on which group is more willing to be led by the Spirit of truth, who was given to lead us into all truth and therefore out of all error.

8

PROPHECY

All evangelicals and most charismatics are agreed that the Bible is (and not just 'contains') the word of God. They are convinced about its divine inspiration and therefore its divine authority. They believe in a God who can speak, has spoken and has enabled what he wants us all to hear to be accurately remembered and recorded in written form by a variety of human agents.

This is not to believe that the biblical writers were mere word processors. Their different temperaments and style affect their writings – but this in no way prevents God from saying exactly what he wants to say through them. Nor is it to believe that all subsequent translations are infallible (not even the version 'authorised' by King James!). Above all, it is not to believe that our interpretations (exegesis) and applications (hermeneutics) carry the same inspiration or authority.

We are 'the people of the Book' (or, rather, of the Books, since there are sixty-six; *biblia* was originally plural and can be translated as 'library'). We have a collection of writings which is definitive for all matters of belief and behaviour. It is a closed 'canon' (or rule), consisting of those writings recognised as communicating the original prophetic and apostolic revelations from God (there were many others not so recognised). It must neither be added to nor subtracted from (Revelation 22:18f has perhaps a wider application than its immediate context).

But the question remains: does God still speak today? Has he been dumb since the canon of scripture was completed? Does he only 'speak' now through the written word? Or indirectly through internal feelings or external circumstances? Or does he still speak as he did before and during the writing of the Bible – with actual words on human lips? In a word, through 'prophesying' and 'prophets'?

Nothing scares some evangelicals more than hearing a charismatic say: 'Thus saith the Lord . . . .' The scriptural phrase (appearing three thousand, eight hundred and eight times in the Old Testament) and the 'Authorised Version' language appear to be claiming an ability to supplement the Bible with additional material. Their reaction ranges from anxiety to horror.

There is clearly a gap here, caused by misunderstanding on both sides. Each needs to rethink their attitude to the 'spiritual gift' of prophecy.

PROPHECY IS NOT SCRIPTURE

An unfortunate distinction has arisen between *rhema* (the 'now' word of God, spoken in prophecy) and *logos* (the 'then' word of God written in scripture). Whether this is the biblical use of these two Greek words is extremely doubtful.

Another version of this outlook is the idea that the written word cannot be preached unless and until the expositor has felt 'inspired' to do so, unless a passage has thus 'come alive'.

Whether it is articulated in these ways or not, there has been a tendency among charismatics to value a present word from God more highly than his past words, to get more excited about visions than verses, pictures than passages. The speaking in Sunday services has shifted from exposition to exhortation, from prepared tuition to shared intuition.

1 recall preaching in a parish church, while struggling with an infected throat. After expounding some chapters of scripture for an hour, after which my voice went altogether, the presiding vicar asked if anyone in the congregation had a word from the Lord! The first to come forward said he had a 'picture' of a lot of bicycles without chains and asked if anyone could give an interpretation. No one did. After five similar contributions, none of which were commented upon, I hoarsely whispered into the microphone: 'Please go home!' —and the packed church emptied in silence. I learned later

that this 'shock' ending had led a group to engage in earnest prayer until the early hours of the morning!

Of course we must encourage contributions and allow for tentative attempts, as well as mistakes. But in this case there were too many (scripture limits them to two or three at most), they were not interpreted, much less 'weighed and judged' (as each should have been) and they were invited at the wrong stage of the service (when there should have been a corporate response to the main message).

An overemphasis on immediate revelations leads progressively to three distorted views on prophecy, each more dangerous than the last.

First, to see prophecy as an *addition* to the Bible. Few have a loose-leaf Bible in practice, but many do in principle. They collect prophecies, even writing them on the fly-leaf of the Bible or slipping them inside the covers. They study and meditate on these as much and with the same reverence as they would the scriptures themselves. For all practical purposes, they have become 'scripture'.

Second, to see prophecy as an *alternative* to scripture. In a subtle way, perhaps even unconsciously, an interest in current prophecies takes the prior place and the regular, systematic meditation on scripture is neglected. In extreme cases, this leads to an obsessive preoccupation with the 'latest' revelation (which is, of course, constantly changing).

Third, to see prophecy as an *advance* on scripture. That is to believe that a prophetic word or picture is actually better for us than reading the Bible or listening to exposition of it. Many charismatics would protest violently against the charge that this represents their scale of values. Yet, in their gatherings, the quantity of time and the quality of attention given to the two pursuits speaks louder than words.

One reason for an over valuation of prophecy is the failure to observe the biblical directions for handling it. For a start, the amount of it is to be strictly limited – two or three contributions at the most in any one meeting. Even more important, each should be 'weighed carefully by the others' (1 Cor 14:29; it is not clear whether 'others' means other prophets present or the rest of the congregation; the context favours the latter).

This need to 'judge' prophecy highlights one of its main differences from scripture. The inspiration of the latter may be taken for granted; all that needs to be discussed is its interpretation and application. The inspiration of prophecy may not be assumed, indeed, must not be. Its source may be divine, human or even satanic. It can even be a mixture of two influences (I have often observed a pause after the first few sentences of a genuine word in the Spirit, followed by a fleshly expansion, due perhaps to the speaker's feeling that it has not been long enough!). The verb 'weigh carefully' is the same as 'distinguishing spirits' (in 1 Corinthians 12:10).

Even when its genuine inspiration has been established, its interpretation and application still have to be considered. In other words, after any prophetic word time needs to be given to follow it through. After all, if God has taken the trouble to speak directly, it is dishonouring to him not to give the most serious attention to what he has said. It has to be added that many so-called prophecies are so trite and banal that one questions whether God would bother so to speak – though we must allow that prophesying, like preaching and other ministries, has to be learned and will be 'simple' at first. And mistakes will be made by beginners, which we must allow each other to make if we are ever to learn.

Perhaps the reason so many 'prophecies' are allowed and accepted uncritically is that we lack the courage required for confrontation. Even elders are afraid to challenge contributions in case they find themselves opposing what is of God. That is a paralysing phobia rather than a healthy fear. It is much better to protect a congregation from credulity by exercising caution. Even if a challenge or reservation later proves to be mistaken, there will be no loss of confidence if that is honestly acknowledged.

One other difference between prophecy and scripture has often been overlooked. Whereas the written word is of universal application, relevant to all believers at all times in all places, the spoken word is for local application only, for the situation in which it is given. It is for those believers at that time, in that place, and is not appropriate, much less mandatory, for anyone else. Those who collect prophecies from different contexts, or convey prophecies from one context to another, are blurring the boundary between prophecy and scripture.

To conclude, prophecy is a good supplement to scripture but a bad substitute for it. Charismatics need to say this loud and clear, in deeds as well as words. The systematic teaching of the whole Bible must have a prime place in their schedule. Paul exhorted Timothy: 'devote yourself to the public reading of scripture, to preaching and to teaching' (1 Tim 4:13; he was referring to the Old Testament and its application to unbelievers and believers; note that Timothy was initiated into this ministry through a prophetic word; 1 Tim 4:14). When this is done, prophetic ministry is seen in its true perspective and is more effective in its divine purpose of edifying the body of Christ (1 Cor 14:3).

APOSTOLIC IS NOT ABNORMAL

We have already mentioned (in Chapter 5) a kind of thinking ('dispensational') which divides history into distinct ages and tends to separate the apostolic period (recorded in the New Testament) from the rest of church history. The result is that the characteristic experiences of that era are regarded as special, even unique, and therefore not to be taken as normal, or as a standard for the whole of church life in time and space.

Yet the New Testament does not envisage two ages in the history of the church. With Pentecost began the final era, the 'last days', the age of the Spirit. This extends unchanged from the first advent of Christ to the second. From beginning to end its doctrinal basis is to be found in apostolic testimony, unvarying in content though inevitably altered in form from oral to written with the death of the original apostles.

The church is 'built on the foundation of the apostles and prophets' (Eph 2:20; note the definite article). This is often assumed to refer to those who gave us the Old and New Testament scriptures (though one would have expected the order: 'prophets and apostles' in this case). That interpretation cannot be given to the 'apostles' and 'prophets' listed as post-ascension gifts of Christ to his church (Eph 4:11). Are there, then, any apostles and prophets today?

A careful study of the New Testament data reveals five categories of 'apostle'. The word means simply 'sent-one' (from the Greek verb *apostelein*, which means 'to send'; the Latin equivalent is *mittere*, from which we get 'missionary', and 'missile'!). The categories are distinguished by answering three questions: *who* sent them, *where* were they sent from and to, and *why* were they sent?

1. Jesus himself was an apostle (Heb 3:1). Sent by his Father into the world to save mankind, his apostleship was absolutely unique, though we note that he did not begin the task until he was joined by another sent down from heaven, the Holy Spirit (setting a pattern of dual operation).

2. The disciples of Jesus (Matt 10:2) were sent out two by two into Galilee to declare and demonstrate the kingdom (on one occasion with fifty-eight others). But what constituted

them as 'the Twelve' unique apostles was their personal knowledge of Jesus before his death and after his resurrection, qualifying them to testify that it was the same person, as 'witnesses' to his resurrection (Acts 1:21f; 1 Cor 15:5).

3. Paul is in a category by himself, the 'last of all' those who could claim that special commission by an appearance of the risen (and, in his case alone, the ascended) Lord Jesus to be a primary channel of his revelation and thus an author of scripture (1 Cor 9:1f; 15:8; 2 Pet 3:15f). Yet he was also another kind of 'apostle' and bridged the third and fourth classifications.

4. Many others were sent out by the Spirit through the churches, to pioneer in virgin territory and plant new communities of the kingdom. They never travelled singly; each apostolic team had at least two men (and often women). Many are named (Barnabas, Silas, Titus); others remain anonymous (Rom 16:7; 1 Cor 12:29; 2 Cor 8:23).

5. The label could be given to anyone sent anywhere to do anything. The Philippian church sent Epaphroditus to be Paul's general factotum during his house arrest in Rome as their 'apostle' (Phil 2:25; it is a pity that most English translators have shrunk from the word).

From this brief review, it is obvious that the first three categories were non-recurring and are now obsolete. But two types remain and should be gratefully recognised and received. The church must remain 'apostolic', not only with the orthodoxy of the 'primary' apostles (often spelt with a capital 'A'), but also with the mobility of the 'secondary' ones.

Charismatics have sometimes confused, and therefore abused, their concept of apostleship. The milder mistake has seen apostleship in episcopal terms, exercising more or less permanent, translocal oversight of a number of established churches, instead of transferring this responsibility to a local body of elders (Tit 1:5). The more serious error is to take Paul's apostolic authority as a model for today; this invariably leads to a hierarchical structure demanding total submission. Distortions should not be allowed to dismiss the possibility of genuine apostolic ministry of the fourth and fifth categories today. Counterfeiting the obsolete is pointless.

A similar consideration of prophetic ministry is needed, for prophets are frequently listed and linked with apostles in the New Testament. Was prophesying intended to be a continuing gift and prophets a continuing ministry in the church? And if so, what is its function? How can it 'supplement' scripture yet be kept subordinate to it?

All scripture was originally prophecy. God usually spoke to and through human mouthpieces (on a few occasions he produced sound-waves himself, which could be mistaken for thunder, but this was rare; e.g. John 12:28f).

Not all prophecy became scripture. Some examples of false prophecy are included (Jer 6:14; 8:11). Many speakers of true prophecy are excluded (for example, the messages of Obadiah's 'hidden hundred' in the Old Testament and Philip's four daughters in the New; 1 Kgs 18:4; Acts 21:9).

Scripture is therefore an inspired collection of those prophecies which are definitive for our faith, by which all others are to be judged. The selection is complete. It is neither right nor necessary to add any others to this standard revelation.

Yet spoken words continued to be given alongside the written word, both in Israel and the church. We will call one the 'vertical' word, coming down in the present; and the other the 'horizontal' word, coming along from the past. The fact that they persisted together shows that the vertical word of prophecy had more functions than simply becoming the horizontal word of scripture. Both had a role to play. There were many prophecies which were not, and never would be, part of definitive scripture.

Both were called 'the word of God'. King David praised the Lord all through his life for the written word (Psalm 119 is the best, and longest, example); at the end of his life, he thanked the Lord for the spoken word through himself (2 Sam 23:2; this qualified him to be a 'prophet', Acts 2:30).

At times, the prophetic word (often called 'vision') became scarce, even though previous revelation was still available. In the days of Samuel's boyhood 'the word of the Lord was rare; there were not many visions' (1 Sam 3:1). Later, Solomon acutely observed that 'where there is no vision the people perish', which is more accurately translated as: 'where there is no revelation, the people cast off restraint' (Prov 29:18, NIV). The rarely quoted second half of the verse concludes: 'but blessed is he who keeps the law'. In other words, when there is no *present* revelation many people tend to forget God, but at such times the few who seek to live by *past* revelation are still blessed by him. Amos' prediction of 'a famine of hearing the words of God' (Amos 8:11) does not refer to a shortage of scriptures or expositors but an absence of prophetic revelation.

Here are hints of a two-fold function of prophecy: to give a real sense of the presence of the living God and to recall his past revelation by applying it to the contemporary scene. The keynote of prophecy is immediacy. Revelation is made relevant. God is immanent, present with his people, speaking to them.

While prophets applied the general revelation of the past in a vivid way, they also gave particular directions for the present. They were often consulted for guidance in specific situations. What was the right course of action in these circumstances? To 'enquire of the Lord' meant asking a prophet (1 Kgs 18:6). King Jehoshaphat was wise enough to tell his people: 'Have faith in the Lord your God and you will be upheld; have faith in his prophets and you will be successful' (1 Kgs 20:20). The first exhortation covered strategy, the second tactics and both encouraged morale. No wonder the battle was won.

Note that the 'horizontal' word from the past gave general guidance as to *what* must be done, the 'vertical' word in the present gave particular guidance as to *how* it must be done (see Jahaziel's instructions in the case above; 1 Kgs 20:15–17). Jehoshaphat was simply following the example of King David, who habitually 'enquired of the Lord' before going into battle (1 Sam 30:8; 2 Sam 2:1; 5:19, 23).

But there came a day when this was no longer possible. Prophesying ceased; prophets disappeared.

Between Malachi and Matthew there is a gap of four hundred years during which God was silent. There was only the horizontal (written) word of God. Biblical scholarship developed its familiar conservative and liberal wings (Pharisees and Sadducees). Prophets were replaced by scribes.

It was a long wait to hear from God again. No wonder the crowds flocked to John – Elijah Mark II! He was 'a prophet . . . and more than a prophet', the last to appear before the advent of God's anointed Messiah (Matt 11:9f).

Jesus made remarkably few references to scripture (at least until after his resurrection; Luke 24, 27:44f). He did not use the phrase found nearly four thousand times on the lips of Hebrew prophets: 'Thus saith the Lord . . . .' His messages were introduced and interlaced with, 'Verily, verily (in Hebrew *amen, amen*), *I* say to you . . . .' His words came from the Spirit rather than scripture (John 6:63; cf Acts 1:2). He was not only *the* prophet foretold by Moses (Deut 18:18f; John 6:14). He was himself *the* 'vertical' word, direct from heaven, made flesh and 'tabernacling' among men (John 1:14).

Since prophecy, ceasing with Malachi, reappearing in John,

had now reached its ultimate climax in Jesus, in both his person and his message, we might expect that this would mark the end of prophecy, with only a written record afterwards.

Surprisingly, this does not happen. The prophetic stream may narrow down until it is represented as one supreme expression in the person of the Lord Jesus; but after his death, resurrection and ascension, the stream broadens out again to become a river, wider than it had ever been before!

Jesus had spoken about sending 'prophets and wise men and teachers' to his people (Matt 23:34). But it had been anticipated long before that. Moses' wish that all the Lord's people were prophets (Num 11:29) had become a certain expectation with Joel's prediction (Joel 2:28–32).

Pentecost inaugurated the prophethood of all believers. Regardless of age, sex or class, all God's people were now capable of prophesying, having had the Spirit of prophecy 'poured out' upon them.

Direct communications from God characterise the early history of the church. Before Pentecost they resorted to casting lots to discover his will. After Pentecost they are 'told' by the Spirit, 'led' by the Spirit, 'compelled' by the Spirit, 'forbidden' by the Spirit.

The same combination of 'vertical' and 'horizontal' revelation that guided Israel now guided the church. The strategy of their mission came from the present words of the Holy Spirit.

It is necessary to distinguish between the gift of prophecy

and the ministry of a prophet, though the difference is one of degree rather than kind. Prophesying was open to all believers and Paul encouraged everybody to do it, as well as speak in tongues (1 Cor 14:5; a taunting remark if this was not possible). He envisages, though he does not encourage it, a whole congregation prophesying (1 Cor 14:24). He would rather see members prophesying than speaking in tongues (we shall consider his reasons in Chapter 10). As in the Old Testament, prophecy communicates a vivid sense of the immanence of God (1 Cor 14:24f).

Some will exercise this gift more frequently than others and develop it to the point where it becomes their primary function within the body. They are 'prophets', but only some will reach this stage ('Are all prophets?'; 1 Cor 12:29).

Both the gift and the ministry relate to particular situations. The word to set aside and send out Paul and Barnabas for their calling is one example (Acts 13:2; note the presence of 'prophets and teachers'). The predictions of Agabus, one of a whole group of prophets, were quite specific: first of a world-wide famine (11:28; note that it led to a collection of aid before the disaster!), later of Paul's arrest and imprisonment in Jerusalem (Acts 21:10f; note that it did not deter Paul from his intended visit). Who is to say the church does not need such tactical help today?

Was prophecy intended to continue, or have we entered another 'apocryphal' interlude such as that between the Testaments? If so, this is the longest silence of God since

Abraham! No wonder there are so many discussions and publications on how to enquire of the Lord for particular direction. Scripture tells us how to live but not where; how to be married, but not who to; how to do our job, but not what job to do. Why is guidance so complicated for us when it was so simple for them? What does Paul mean when he says that 'those who are led by the Spirit of God are sons of God' (Rom 8:14)?

We have digressed from our study of the New Testament teaching about prophecy, but only to highlight its place in the corporate life of the daily church and its continued usefulness. But was it expected to remain alongside the 'horizontal' written word after it was completed? The evidence is cumulative and may be stated as a series of propositions:

1. Prophets and prophesying are an integral part of church life for the *whole* of the New Testament period (featured in Acts, Romans, 1 Corinthians, Ephesians, 1 & 2 Thessalonians, 1 Timothy).

2. To exclude prophecy leads to an artificial, arbitrary subdivision of passages. Prophecy is included in *all* the lists of gifts and ministries, often in close association with teachers.

3. Nowhere is prophesying directly related to the formation of scripture, though that is clearly linked to the 'primary' apostles.

4. Prophecy is *the* sign of the 'last days', according to Joel and Peter; and the most natural understanding is that it will

characterise the whole of this final era rather than mark its inauguration.

5. There will be false prophets to the end of the age (Matt 24:24; Rev 2:20; 20:10), as well as true (Rev 11:3). Once again, the appearance of the counterfeit implies the presence of the genuine.

6. The only mention of prophecy 'ceasing', dates this at the time when the perfect comes, our knowledge is complete and we see face to face – surely a reference to the end of the age (1 Cor 13:8–12).

7. Scripture anticipates a great increase of prophesying under the new covenant, not a gradual decrease or sudden disappearance.

Adding these seven points together makes a strong case for continued prophecy in the church. Rightly understood and handled, it presents no threat to the completed canon or accepted authority of scripture.

Evangelicals are therefore invited to reconsider the place of 'apostles and prophets' alongside the other gifts of 'evangelists, pastors and teachers', since they are all grouped together in scripture, without any hint that the church would soon lose two of them (Eph 4:11). At the same time, charismatics need to make sure that the 'restoration' of apostolic and prophetic ministries is strictly in accord with the biblical definition of their function and directions for their exercise.

9

INITIATION

In this chapter we are going to consider what is probably the most critical difference between charismatics and evangelicals, and the one over which there may be the greatest reluctance to reconsider traditional positions. Both streams need to ask whether they have done full justice to the New Testament data.

The issue is nothing less than the fundamental question: what is a Christian and how does anyone become one? There is already a very wide range of answers, the definitions varying from 'baptised' to 'born again' and the process being described in a host of ways:

'deciding to follow Jesus',
'asking him into your life',
'making a commitment',

'opening the door to him',

'joining the church',

'receiving him into your heart',

'giving your life to him',

'inviting him in'.

However, to focus on the tension we must face in this chapter, we shall begin with the two greatest gifts of God at the heart of the gospel: the 'objective' gift of his Son to take away our sins and the 'subjective' gift of his Spirit to give us his holiness.

There is good ground in scripture for defining a Christian as someone who has accepted both gifts from God – by believing in the Son and receiving the Spirit. The latter is the 'seal', the proof, the confirmation that a person has been forgiven and accepted by God into his family (Acts 15:8; Eph 1:13; 1 John 4:13).

So far, so good. Both streams would agree on that last paragraph until further questions are asked about what it actually means in practice.

How and when is the Spirit 'received'? To put it another way: how do believing in the Son and receiving the Spirit relate to each other? Are they but two aspects of the same event or can one happen without the other?

I have devoted an entire book to this matter of initiation (*The Normal Christian Birth*, Hodder and Stoughton, 1989). Much of this chapter is a condensation, though not a straight

repetition, of that volume and those who wish to explore the subject in greater depth are recommended to read it. It offers a point of integration which is in between charismatic and evangelical but is claimed to be more biblical than either. Both streams are urged to rethink their assumptions.

RECEIVING IS NOT REPEATED

All charismatics believe in a self-evident experience of the Spirit, though they may use different terms to describe it. Some call it the 'baptism', others the 'fullness' of the Spirit.

They will talk about 'receiving the baptism' or 'receiving the fullness'. But they are, surprisingly, very reluctant to use the phrase 'receiving the Spirit' to describe this event. That is because most charismatics have been taught that receiving the gift of the Spirit happens at another time and in another way, prior to being baptised in or filled with the Spirit. It is usually assumed that the gift was received unconsciously and without outward manifestation, either when the sacrament of baptism was administered (the Catholic view) or when faith in Christ was first professed (the evangelical view).

This separates the 'baptism' or 'fullness' from initiation and makes it a sequel, a 'second' step. It has even been called '*the* second blessing'. In other words, whatever terms are used, the clear inference is that our relationship with the Holy Spirit is established in *two stages*. This is inevitably taken to imply

that there are two 'classes' of Christians: the 'first class' who rejoice that they have passed both stages and the 'second class' who resent being told they haven't! This is often regarded as the most offensive feature of charismatic thought.

Some, mainly pentecostals, use the word 'receive' of both the initial and subsequent events. The first 'reception' of the Spirit is said to be 'for *salvation*' and takes place automatically and usually subconsciously at the moment of conversion (which is what most evangelicals believe). The second 'reception' of the Spirit is said to be 'for *service*' and is a self-evident 'baptism' with supernatural power for the release of spiritual gifts (which some evangelicals believe but many do not). Those who teach two 'receptions' usually insist on tongues as the necessary evidence of the second (see Chapter 10).

The problem with this whole line of thinking is that the New Testament knows nothing of two receptions of the Spirit in the life of the believer. There is only one reception of the gift of the Spirit, offered to all who repent and are baptised (Acts 2:38).

Furthermore, a careful comparison of the terms used shows that 'received' is used synonymously with 'baptised' and 'filled' (the reader is invited to check this out in such verses as John 7:39; Acts 1:5; 2:4; 10:47; 11:15f; 19:2–6). To 'receive' the Spirit was exactly the same as to be 'baptised' and 'filled' – and to be 'sealed' and to have had the Spirit 'poured out' (Eph 1:13; Tit 3:5). It is quite impossible to force these terms

into two separate occasions; they are used interchangeably of the one event.

There is only one text which might be used in this way. In the 'upper room' on the first Easter Sunday, 'Jesus breathed (literally, blew) on his disciples and said, "Receive Holy Spirit"' (John 20:22). Some have claimed that this was their first reception for salvation, while the second for service came two months later at Pentecost. There are many difficulties with this interpretation. The disciples were already born again, regenerate (John 1:12; 13:10). Thomas was not present, so missed it. Nothing is recorded to have happened as a result. The event was apparently of no importance to Matthew, Mark or Luke. The coming of the Spirit was dependent on Jesus' departure which had not yet taken place (John 16:7). Above all, Peter always referred to Pentecost as the occasion when he 'received' the Spirit (Acts 10:47; 11:17; 15:9). It seems fair to see this incident as a 'proleptic' preparation, a rehearsal for Pentecost. He gave them a sign (his breath or wind) and a command to respond ('Receive' is in the imperative mood). Note that the command came after the sign; the order would have been the reverse if he was actually imparting the Spirit to them then.

So charismatics must stop thinking (and talking) in two-stage terms. The single reception/baptism/filling is an integral part of the first blessing, not a later one. It should normally come right at the beginning of the Christian life. It is, however, distinct from simply believing in Jesus, as we will explore more fully in the second half of this chapter. In the New Testament this filling was usually just after baptism, as with Jesus, once just before, as with Cornelius, but never during. A delay was abnormal, as in the case of the Samaritans. Its absence caused immediate concern and was rectified as soon as possible, as at Samaria and Ephesus.

It is also clear that this single reception was not just for service to others but was necessary for their own salvation. Life in the kingdom was life in the Spirit. Righteousness, peace and joy were dependent on his indwelling (Rom 14:17). The personal and powerful presence of the Holy Spirit is both the proof of justification and the prerequisite of sanctification (Rom 8:1–9).

In separating the 'reception' of the Spirit into two stages, charismatics have made the baptism/filling into an optional extra, as far as salvation is concerned. It is no longer essential for citizenship in the kingdom of heaven; at most it will only gain an enlarged reward for more effective service. Such thinking is far removed from the New Testament, where Pentecost is the characteristic sign of the 'last days', the new age when the kingdom has come with power. The possession of the Spirit is the mark of those who have entered and enjoyed the kingdom which is yet to come in its full manifestation. Their lives will be identified by purity and power because they have received the Holy Spirit of God himself.

BELIEVING IS NOT RECEIVING

This is probably the hardest thing for evangelicals to learn in the whole of this book. For it is a matter of practice as well as principle, underlying their evangelistic methods, particularly in counselling enquirers.

In a word, they firmly believe that believing in Jesus and receiving the Spirit are one and the same thing, that they happen at exactly the same moment and may or may not be self-evident. All that is required is a profession of repentance and faith (usually in the form of standardised words known as 'the sinner's prayer'). Those who take this 'step' are then assumed, on the basis of selected texts, to have been 'born' of the Spirit and to have 'received the Spirit' (though the latter is rarely mentioned). The whole process is usually quite unrelated to being 'baptised', in water or in Holy Spirit (those who claim they have been 'baptised' in Spirit only say this in theological debate and not to the converts themselves; and they would never say they were 'filled' at this point).

Confused thinking is revealed both in the texts and terms used in such evangelistic counselling. I have studied a few dozen manuals for counsellors and booklets for enquirers and found two verses which are used (and misused!) far more than any others. One is 'Behold, I stand at the door and knock; if any man hears my voice and opens the door, I will come in and sup with him and he with me' (Rev 3:20). This has nothing whatever to do with conversion. The door belongs to a successful church of believers who are unaware of having lost the presence of Christ; the prophetic word invites any member to remedy the situation. When misapplied to individual conversion, two wrong conclusions are drawn. First, becoming a Christian is reduced to the single step of 'inviting him in', which ignores the real nature of faith, to say nothing of repentance or baptism. Second, it disguises the real situation: it is the sinner who is outside the door needing to knock and it is the Saviour's decision to open it (indeed, he himself is the door).

The other is 'Yet to all who received him, to those who believed in his name, he gave the right (the word is *exousia*, 'authority'; not *dunamis*, 'power') to become children of God' (John 1:12). The past tense of the verbs is ignored, yet this is the key to the meaning and application of this verse. The context confirms that it is an historical statement referring to the time when Jesus was on the earth among his own Jewish people. Some did not 'receive' him, but others did. This was the pattern right up to his death. But, after his ascension, when the heavens 'received' him back, that verb was never used of him again. It was transferred from the second person of the Trinity to the third, who had taken his place on earth. He will only be received again down here when he returns.

New Testament evangelists exhorted their hearers to *repent* towards God for their sins, *believe* in the Lord Jesus Christ as their Saviour and *receive* the gift of the Holy Spirit. Their converts had a trinitarian relationship with God from the beginning.

Modern evangelists (who are mostly evangelical) rarely use this threefold invitation. There is less emphasis on a repentance that is expressed in deed as well as word (Luke 3:8; Acts 26:20). The second and third items are run together into '*receive Jesus* as your Saviour and Lord'. To question this might seem to some a verbal quibble. But the phraseology reflects the evangelical assumption that believing in Jesus and receiving the Spirit are one and the same thing.

The evidence of the New Testament is that they can and ought to be distinguished from each other, that they may be separated in time, that it is necessary to make sure that both have happened and possible to know that they have.

The original disciples, of course, believed in Jesus long before they received the Spirit (John 7:39). But that can be explained by the transitional pre-Pentecostal nature of their situation. The Spirit was 'not yet' (English translations add 'given' to amplify this unusual statement, which clearly refers to the Spirit's availability, rather than his existence).

Even one case *after* Pentecost of the separation in time between believing and receiving, would be enough to demonstrate their distinction. And there is such an example in Samaria (Acts 8:16); they believed in Jesus without receiving the Spirit, which shows that it is *possible* to have one without the other. Some scholars have tried to prove they were not true

147

believers, but Peter and John would not have agreed with that diagnosis. Paul's question to the Ephesian disciples reveals that he also accepted the possibility of believing without receiving, even though he did later discover that they did not yet have full personal faith in Jesus (Acts 19:1–6).

In any case, Paul led them to faith in Jesus and baptised them in water into his name *before* they received the Spirit, so the gap in time is still there, though much briefer than with the Samaritans. Furthermore, this seems to have been the usual pattern for the majority of early converts: water baptism came *between* believing in Jesus and receiving the Spirit.

Moreover, the gift of the Spirit and its reception is associated with prayer and the laying-on of hands. Jesus himself had received while praying after his baptism in the river Jordan (Luke 3:21f). He encouraged others to do the same: 'how much more will your Father in heaven give Holy Spirit to those who go on asking him' (Luke 11:13; there is no definite article and the last verb is in the present continuous tense). This encouragement would be inappropriate for unbelievers, since the 'world cannot receive' the Spirit (John 14:17); but it would be unnecessary for believers if they have already received! The fact is that prayer was made for believers to receive, together with that intensified expression of intercession, the laying-on of hands (Acts 8:17f; 9:17; 19:6; 2 Tim 1:6f; Heb 6:2).

One of the main differences between believing in Jesus and receiving the Spirit is that the evidence for the former is human action (in fruits of repentance and submission to baptism), whereas evidence for the latter is divine action. In studying all the recorded receptions of the Spirit, it is impossible not to conclude that every time there was an audible/visible manifestation that God had fulfilled 'the promise'. His gift was obvious and was described in vivid phrases: the Spirit had 'come upon', had 'fallen on', been 'poured out upon' (language familiar to any Jew who knew the Old Testament). To be 'baptised' (immersed, plunged, dipped) in Holy Spirit was as definite an experience as being baptised in water.

It was the absence of such an event in the experience of the Samaritan believers which clearly showed they had not received the Spirit, 'because the Holy Spirit had not yet *come upon* them' (Acts 8:16). Two logical inferences from this statement are seldom drawn. First, immediate corroboration was expected; they did not wait for 'fruit' to appear. Second, if the absence of such an experience was taken as proof that the Spirit had not been received, then every other believer up till then must have had that experience. It was only the delay that made the Samaritans abnormal. Their reception was typical, obvious enough for Simon to be impressed, though what he saw is not specified (Acts 8:18).

Evangelicals, therefore, will have to look again at their assumptions about how and when the Spirit is 'received' (in the New Testament sense of that verb, synonymous with 'baptised' and 'filled') and come to terms with the uniform testimony that this is a definite and discernible occurrence in its own right.

* * * * *

Both charismatics and evangelicals shrink from the pastoral implications of making these doctrinal adjustments. In this hesitation, they are both in danger of allowing their experience to override theology!

The problem is simply stated. If the reception/baptism/filling of the Spirit is *both* an integral element in Christian initiation and a discernible experience, then many professing Christians, in some churches most, have *not* 'received' the Holy Spirit. That conclusion would have to be drawn, if the New Testament meaning has been truly defined above. The crisis that would be precipitated for many pastors by thinking such thoughts, never mind preaching them, discourages an objective reappraisal. Charismatics escape the dilemma by separating 'received' from 'baptised' (or repeating 'received'), while evangelicals escape by separating 'baptised' from 'filled' (and by using the static nouns – 'baptism' and 'fulness' – where scripture uses dynamic verbs).

Such reluctance to give words their scriptural meaning indicates that much more is at stake than an agreed etymology to avoid double-talk. The real concern is the spiritual state and status of those who, by this definition, have not received the Spirit. Does this mean that they are not 'saved'? If they die before 'receiving', will they not go to heaven?

There are many hidden assumptions in such questions (for example, that 'saved' means safe from hell rather than salvaged from sins). They tend to be framed in terms of death and the next world rather than life in this one. They need to be patiently unravelled before being given a slick answer, for a question can be 'loaded' with a doubtful premise. Let me offer a few tentative suggestions for resolving this emotive debate.

First, salvation is a process: we have been saved from the penalty of sin (justification), we are being saved from the power of sin (sanctification) and we shall be saved from the presence of sin (glorification). The first name, and the best, for Christianity was 'the Way'. It is a road to be travelled, which begins with repentance and ends in heaven. The vital thing is to be 'on the way' and moving forward. If someone dies near the beginning of their pilgrimage (for example, before they could be baptised in water or Spirit) they were already 'on the way' and I believe would be with the Lord.

The problem is not those who die before they have travelled very far but those who live and don't travel at all, those who mistakenly think that they have 'arrived' rather than set out. To be salvaged from their sins in this life, they need everything God has offered to them, including baptism in water and Spirit (John 3:5; Tit 3:3). If they don't 'receive' the Spirit, they are in a vulnerable, even dangerous, state – precisely because his power and purity are essential to a clean walk through this dirty world.

But there is more to be said. Are they entirely 'without' the Spirit? At the risk of being accused of returning to the familiar 'two-stage' theology of the Spirit, I want to suggest that the 'reception' of the Spirit is not the beginning of a believer's relationship with him, though it will then become a conscious relationship. The change is one of degree rather than kind.

Certainly it was for the first disciples. They had believed in Jesus and performed healings and exorcisms in his name from time to time, unaware that the power to do so came from the same Spirit who had anointed Jesus. In preparing them for the coming of his replacement, the Comforter ('Standby' would be a better translation), he told them: 'You know him, for he lives *with* you and will be *in* you' (John 14:17; note the change of preposition). The significant point to notice is that 'receive' was applied to the moment when the Spirit took up residence *within* them, not to his earlier presence *with* them (John 7:39).

From one point of view, their situation was unique, in that they believed in Jesus *before* his death, resurrection, ascension and sending of the Spirit. Nevertheless, there is something of a parallel in the experience of all later believers. The very first stirrings of conviction about such realities as sin, righteousness and judgement are due to the work of the Holy Spirit (John 16:8). It is he who makes the truths about Jesus convincing and makes possible repentance and faith. No penitent, baptised believer could have got that far without him (even the Samaritans in Acts 8). The conclusion drawn above does not deny that the Holy Spirit is already working on the life of anyone finding 'the Way', which is Christ himself (John 14:6).

But it is confusing and misleading to call this work of the Spirit 'receiving' or 'having' the Spirit, much less saying he 'indwells' them. This is to leave them satisfied (or unsatisfied) with less than their full heritage. It is to send them into the battles ahead without the full resources available to them. It is a failure to give them a conscious relationship with their great 'Standby'.

At the very least, new believers need to be sure that God has forgiven and adopted them. A syllogistic argument from a verse of scripture ('The Bible says it – you believe it – that settles it') is no substitute for that inward assurance of the Spirit that makes us cry out loud (Rom 8:15f; the Greek verb *krazein* means 'to call out involuntarily'; cf Matt 14:26). One of the most noticeable differences in the disciples after they received the Spirit at Pentecost was their courage, their boldness in speaking out (Acts 4:13, 31).

Many who make 'decisions' for Christ, 'invite him into their lives' and 'make a commitment to him', later fall away. They are then much more difficult to recover. It is a concern in all evangelism. Could it be that a major cause of this tragedy is our failure to make sure that they have repented toward God, believed in Jesus and 'received'; been 'baptised in' and 'filled with' the Holy Spirit? Should we let our fear of reactions within the church to the recovery of apostolic preaching and practice prevent us from offering to those outside of Christ all that he died to make possible?

10

GLOSSOLALIA

'Tongues' is a horrid word. It conjures up an impression of uncontrolled speech at best, meaningless babble at worst. Loose talk of any kind is abhorred in polite society, especially under the influence of alcohol. 'Speaking in tongues' has been associated with such embarrassing outbursts since the day of Pentecost (Acts 2:13).

The Greek word (*glossa*) means simply 'language' and it is a great pity it has not been translated that way in English versions of the Bible (NIV gives 'languages' in the margin as an alternative). This limits its content to articulate speech, with syntax and grammar. Jesus discouraged gibberish: 'And when you pray, do not keep on babbling like pagans, for they think they will be heard because of their many words' (Matt 6:7; the Greek verb is *battologeo* meaning speech that does not communicate, from stammering to pointless repetition).

Prayer is measured by quality rather than quantity, depth rather than length.

However, the almost universal use of 'tongues' rather than 'languages' to describe this spiritual gift compels its adoption in this chapter, though readers are urged to overlook its less helpful connotations – though it has to be admitted that some charismatics have encouraged this misunderstanding by applying the label to what is obviously jabbering and not 'another language'.

The gift of 'tongues' has received publicity out of all proportion to the other spiritual gifts. Perhaps this is due to its being the most obvious difference between charismatics and others – or perhaps because it is the most eccentric and least understood of their characteristic practices. Critics of pentecostalism have described it as 'the tongues movement'.

Charismatics are prone to make too much of tongues and evangelicals are inclined to make too little. One stream tends to use the gift too much in public, the other shrinks from even using it in private. Both need to recover attitudes and action which reflect the biblical balance.

TONGUES ARE NOT EVERYTHING

In giving this material verbally in seminars, I have found that many charismatics, particularly those calling themselves 'pentecostals', find this section the most difficult to accept. I ask for their patience and willingness to check their reactions with the scriptures cited. Though their movement is comparatively recent, there has been time to develop their own cherished traditions, which may not contain the whole truth.

In particular, there are two assumptions which may be questioned in the light of the New Testament.

'Tongues are the evidence of baptism in Spirit.'

Certainly in the majority of recorded cases, tongues figure prominently, supremely on the day of Pentecost itself and on a number of subsequent occasions (Acts 2:4; 10:46; 19:6). It is legitimate to conclude that this was a frequent manifestation, even the usual one; and may be expected to continue to be.

However, to change the indefinite to the definite article ('an' evidence to 'the' evidence) may be a small step in linguistics, but is a giant leap in theology. To regard tongues as 'the initial evidence' (a common, but unbiblical phrase) seems to go beyond the biblical data. It is one thing to say that tongues *may* accompany the reception of the Spirit (and may do so often) and quite another to say they *must*. The following points need to be considered:

First, there are occasions when tongues are not specifically included (Acts 8:17). To be fair, they are not excluded either and something unusual happened to capture the attention of an onlooker (Acts 8:18).

Second, other 'symptoms' are included in the record. For example, in addition to tongues there is praise (Acts 10:46) and prophecy (Acts 19:6), both of which are in known language. It is not entirely clear whether all spoke in 'unknown languages' and their own, or whether some spoke in tongues while others praised or prophesied. Both interpretations are possible, though the latter is slightly more likely.

Third, Paul expressed the wish that all the Corinthian believers spoke in tongues (1 Cor 14:5). This seems an unlikely expression if they had all already done so when they were baptised in one Spirit (1 Cor 12:13). Again, the language is not conclusive, since he may be referring to the continued exercise of the gift (as he certainly is when he asks the rhetorical question, 'Do all speak in tongues?', which does not exclude their once having done so; 1 Cor 12:30).

Fourth, the ending of Mark lists 'speaking in new tongues' among the 'signs that will accompany those who believe' (Mark 16:17; the fact that it may well be a later addition does not necessarily exclude it from the canon of scripture and certainly reflects the expectations of the early church). Yet it obviously means that *any* believer *could* do this rather than that *every* believer *should*, as with drinking poison or handling snakes.

Fifth, since all this data contains an element of ambiguity, what is needed to clinch the matter is an explicit statement that tongues is the evidence for baptism in Spirit. However, such a plain affirmation is conspicuous by its absence. In view of the importance of this issue, which profoundly affects the life of every believer, the silence is significant. In the absence of specific statements, it is dangerous to build doctrine on inference, however logical it may seem ('double predestination' to heaven and hell is a notorious example).

We conclude that it is wrong for charismatics to insist that unless a person has spoken in tongues there has not been a genuine 'baptism' or 'filling'. They may be motivated by a desire to maintain their identity with this distinctive emphasis or, more likely, a fear that the nature of the event will be compromised by lack of definition. If *anything* is accepted as evidence, it will not be long before *nothing* is required or expected (which is the traditional evangelical teaching that the Spirit's 'fulness' is received 'by faith', meaning that a person must believe this has been given whether anything happens or not).

Charismatics are justified in insisting on the definiteness of the event, as *immediately* apparent to recipient and spectator alike. As has been argued already, unless this was universally the case in the early church, no one would have been in a position to say that the baptised believers in Samaria had not received the Spirit (Acts 8:16).

And they are right to expect that the inward experience will be confirmed by outward evidence. To be filled is to reach the point of overflow. A whole strand of biblical teaching encourages the expectation that whatever fills the heart will overflow from the mouth. After all, the Spirit is the Spirit of prophecy. His coming on people in the old covenant led to spontaneous speech, whether intelligible or unintelligible (1 Sam 10:6); the only difference is that in the new covenant all will prophesy rather than some, the ordinary people, not just special persons.

'Prophecy' can be used in a wider sense to cover *any* directly inspired utterance emanating from the divine Spirit. For Peter on the day of Pentecost, tongues were a form of 'prophesying' ('This is that', Acts 2:16), but were not the only possible one. Spontaneous praise or prophecy (in its narrower sense), in a known language, were clearly accepted under the same category.

It seems valid, then, to expect some form of prophesying, in its widest sense, as evidence that the 'promise' has been fulfilled and the 'gift' received. Tongues, which have been 'set on fire by hell' (Jas 3:6), are now at the service of heaven. It is significant that the majority of 'spiritual gifts' (*charismata*) are connected with speech (five out of nine in 1 Corinthians 12:8–10). The witness of the Spirit is more ejaculation than intuition (Rom 8:15; Gal 4:6). Those who are filled with Holy Spirit speak with boldness (Acts 4:31). God uses words to accomplish his purposes of creation and redemption.

'Tongues are the evidence of worship in Spirit.'
In moving from the place of tongues in the life of the individual to their corporate use in the meetings of the church we
touch delicate matters on which many are very sensitive.

While Paul was grateful that he used his gift of tongues
more than all (not just any!) of the Corinthians (1 Cor 14:18),
he chose to do so in private rather than in public (1 Cor 14:19).
However, he did not discourage others from contributing to a
meeting in this way, even coming ready to do so (1 Cor 14:26).
But the public exercise of the gifts must be restrained within
strict limits – only two, or at the most three, such items in
any one gathering and only then if there is prior knowledge of
someone present with the gift of interpretation, able to convey
the content to the rest of the people in their own language.

The principles behind these restrictions are crucial to the
interpretation and application of this whole chapter; there
are two, closely related to each other. First, the primary
concern in corporate worship is not the expression of one's
own devotion to the Lord but the edification of others, helping
them to worship him. Second, their spirits can only be reached
through their minds, which means everything has to be
intelligible to them before it can be edifying. A tongue cannot
edify the speaker unless and until it is rendered intelligible
by interpretation to the listeners.

So far charismatics would agree in theory, though they
are not always consistent in practice. But they react with

indignation when reminded about Paul's application of these principles to the *corporate* use of the gift of tongues, as distinct from its expression by an individual in public.

Clearly, if all present, or even many, use tongues simultaneously, intelligible interpretation is a logistic impossibility. Mutual edification is ruled out; therefore the practice must also be forbidden, not only for this negative omission, but also because of the positive offence it can be to those unable to participate. There are two categories likely to attend 'public' services whose integration could be damaged by such thoughtless activity. On the one side are 'uninitiated' believers, who either do not understand what is happening or have not yet experienced the gift and are unable to participate. On the other side are interested unbelievers, seeking to understand more about the Christian faith and life, who would assume that the people were 'out of their mind' (1 Cor 14:23), which, in a sense, they are (1 Cor 14:14); until the unbeliever discovers that they are in full control of their spirits, it is entirely credible that he jumps to the wrong conclusion, since that dimension is still beyond his grasp. So there is an evangelistic as well as an edificatory aspect to this prohibition.

In spite of this, 'singing in the Spirit' has become a prominent feature of charismatic worship, even its hallmark ('this is what we do that others don't do'). The impression is given that this is the goal and peak of 'a time of worship'. A sequence of loud choruses (called 'praise'), followed by quieter songs (called 'worship'), invariably leads into singing in tongues. Some choruses are known and used to effect the transition ('For Thou, O Lord, art high above all the earth', with its repetition of 'I exalt Thee' is a classic example); nor is it unknown for the musicians to launch into a standard beat which is intended to stimulate singing in tongues (though the instrumentalists rarely participate vocally).

What would Paul think (and say) about all this? How can it be justified in the light of his teaching? Many have never questioned the practice in this way, assuming that if so many sincere people do it, then it must be alright. Those who have thought about it, usually after accepting its validity, have come up with a number of arguments in its favour.

Some draw a distinction between 'speaking' and 'singing' in tongues. Paul certainly mentions both, though he is referring to his private practice (1 Cor 14:15). It is also true that his strictures only mention everyone 'speaking' in tongues (1 Cor 14:23). But is this 'rightly dividing the word of truth' (2 Tim 2:15)? Does something that is wrong when spoken become right when sung? Has the music made such a radical difference? How does a melodic expression overcome the objection that the unintelligible is unedifying?

To this, some would reply that in a musical form tongues can edify, citing cases of unbelievers who have been 'impressed' by hearing it. It is certainly true that it can attract as well as repel. Harmony has an aesthetic appeal in its own right (an opera can be enjoyed by those who speak no Italian). But is such empathy what Paul means by edification? Does it solve his basic problem with unintelligible worship?

Others would quote Paul against himself with a statement from the very same chapter: 'Tongues, then, are a sign, not for believers but for unbelievers' (1 Cor 14:22). Without asking what this sign actually 'signifies' to unbelievers and ignoring Paul's surprising conclusion that tongues should not be used when unbelievers are present, this verse (really half a verse) is taken out of context and used to justify 'singing in the Spirit'. The verse has been a notorious difficulty for teachers and translators (J.B. Philips actually reversed the words to make it say the exact opposite). However, a careful reading reveals that Paul is quite consistent in his conclusion. Tongues are a sign of *rejection* to unbelievers and therefore not to be used in their presence without interpretation (for a detailed exegesis of this passage, see Appendix B). Prophecy which they can understand is much more likely to communicate spiritual benefit and draw them to God and his people (1 Cor 14:24f).

Behind Paul's stance is the understanding that all gifts are to be exercised in love (1 Cor 14:1), which is the 'more excellent way' (1 Cor 12:31). Without this caring concern for others, the exercise of gifts achieves nothing (1 Cor 13:1–3). Such expression is little better than exhibitionism, 'thoughtless' in every sense of the word. God-centred services (of worship or welfare) are other-centred, not self-centred.

Charismatic insistence on corporate tongues in public

meetings discourages many evangelicals from sharing in them. Their reservations may not be entirely dismissed as matters of taste, tradition or temperament. They may be genuinely concerned about their validity in the light of scripture. But they, too, may need to rethink their attitude to the gift of tongues, even if it is confined to individual expression, whether in private or public.

TONGUES ARE NOT NOTHING

Forgive the grammar, but the double negative seemed a good way to express the obverse of the previous section!

If charismatics have focused too much attention on tongues, evangelicals have done the exact opposite, at least for most of their history (the picture has changed in recent years).

The subject has been studiously avoided or instantly dismissed. Some fellowships have dared to forbid the public exercise of tongues altogether, in spite of the clear command in scripture not to do so (1 Cor 14:39). It has even been ascribed to Satan, which comes dangerously near to committing the unforgivable sin (Matt 12:24, 32). It is widely assumed that it is an unnecessary function within the body, somewhat akin to the appendix, which only causes trouble when it makes its presence known! We can get on very well without it, perhaps even better. In attitude if not in articulation, the impression is given that God really should not have chosen this gift to mark the 'birthday of the church' and was not very wise in perpetuating it afterwards.

Some of this is due to sheer ignorance, or at least a failure to study its place in scripture. There is considerable misunderstanding of what the gift is and does. There is more information in the Bible than many realise.

The first example comes very early, at the tower of Babel (from which our word 'babble' is derived). God gave immediate ability to speak different languages. This was not inarticulate 'babbling', but it did sound like it to those who had only known and spoken one language. However, this gift was a sign of rejection, an expression of God's judgement on their godlessness (as it was to be later to Israel in the time of Isaiah; note that Isaiah 28:11f is also quoted in 1 Corinthians 14:21 – see Appendix B). The result of this was confusion (the Hebrew word for 'confused' sounds like 'Babel') and separation (Gen 11:7f).

By contrast, the result of the same gift on the day of Pentecost was to draw people together rather than drive them apart, to promote rather than prevent understanding. It was the sign chosen by God to signal the dawn of a new era, the establishment of a new covenant, of spirit rather than letter (2 Cor 3:6). That the tongues were real languages is confirmed by those who heard and recognised them. Why should this be thought a strange miracle for a God who understands and speaks all languages, because he gave them all?

Many evangelicals would be happier if God had stopped

there. Such a dramatic action seems appropriate to such a significant event. Why continue it as a perpetuated feature of church life? After all, it's much easier to believe in and cope with tongues in the historical past than in the existential present!

Yet it did continue. There is as much space given to directions for its use (and against its abuse) as with the Lord's Supper, the central feature of Christian worship down through the centuries. It cannot be dismissed (as has been attempted with other spiritual gifts) as necessary to attest apostolic testimony until the canon of scripture was completed, since its public exercise was restricted and even discouraged.

It has been deliberately devalued before it is dismissed. Some argue that its bottom position in the list of spiritual gifts means that it is the 'least' important of them; actually, it is not the last and this argument is never applied to 'self-control' which is bottom of the list of the fruit of the Spirit (1 Cor 12:10; Gal 5:23). Others take Paul's restrictions on its public use as an indication that he would be happier without it, which ignores his gratitude for its benefits to himself and his wish that all others could know the same (evangelicals would do well to ask themselves why they do not share his sentiments).

True, the gift has been misused; Corinth is not the only place where it has got out of hand. But of what gift or ministry could not the same be said? Has there not been 'bad experience' of immoral evangelists, incompetent pastors and incoherent teachers? But this has never been used to deny all such ministries. Why are tongue-speakers treated differently?

Our appraisal must begin with the fact that tongues are given by God, and therefore one of those 'good and perfect gifts from above' (Jas 1:17). To belittle it is to demean its source. It is a gift of grace, a *charisma*, to be received with gratitude. It is one of those things which believers are allowed, even exhorted, to 'covet' (1 Cor 14:1)! There should be an eagerness, not just a willingness, to receive it.

Why? What use is it? What value has it? We can mention at least four, in the order in which they may be experienced.

First, it is an evidence of having received the Spirit. We have already seen that it is the most frequently mentioned manifestation of this event in the New Testament. It may be expected to be the same today, though we have concluded that it is wrong to insist that it must be so in every case. The free flow of a new language is both liberating and confirmatory, bringing an immediate assurance that the Spirit has taken up residence.

Second, it is an edifying gift. It builds up the speaker in spiritual strength and resources. One wonders how often Paul used it to recover from imprisonment, beatings, stonings and other sufferings. It is the one gift given to edify one's self rather than others, though it can do that also, when teamed with the gift of interpretation (1 Cor 14:4f).

Third, it is a real help in praising God and praying for others. Most of us get 'stuck for words' or simply 'don't know what to say'. So the God who wants us to have intercourse with him and to make intercession for others comes to our aid, allowing our spirit to communicate without the limitations of our own thought-processes. The mind is unfruitful, that is, unproductive while this gift is being used (1 Cor 14:14). This allows mental relaxation (a blessing in itself!) or concentration on other things at the same time (it is the safest form of prayer while driving!).

Fourth, it is *a* (not *the*) gateway to other gifts. It is very 'good for starters'. It can be tried out on one's self before risking it on others. It builds up confidence in the supernatural ability to go beyond natural ability ('I can do things I could never have done before'). To know the blessing one gift can bring to one's self is to desire to have other gifts to bless others. For many, tongues has been the introduction to a whole new range of possibilities.

Who would not want such a gift? Any fellowship would be enriched by it. If it is not 'earnestly desired', even if it is not immediately bestowed, there is something wrong.

11

WORSHIP

We must now consider the very practical area of tension and conflict felt in corporate worship. Many would understand 'charismatic' as referring to a particular style of worship. Some evangelicals find it so repugnant that they feel unable to attend public meetings of this kind.

Part of this may simply be attributed to the normal aversion of traditionalists to novelty. The rate of change has been very rapid. And we need to understand that in a world in which so much is changing, many have found their emotional security in a religion that is changeless, even though they have failed to distinguish between its eternal principles and the application of these to contemporary culture.

There is also a 'generation gap' to consider. Actually, we should be talking about 'gaps'. Fashion cycles (in music, clothes, language, etc.) are over in less than four years.

Keeping up with them is just one more source of stress in modern society. The Reformation principle of communicating the gospel in the culture of the people is a good deal harder to apply today than it was then! If the church is to avoid becoming a dwindling club for pensioners, worship services have to be adapted to the cultural contexts of the people she seeks to serve and win. God himself did this in the incarnation.

But it would be a major mistake to assume that the differences over worship are entirely questions of cultural adaptation. There are theological factors as well.

Worship is the highest activity of which human beings are capable. It is bound to reflect their convictions about the God they worship and their understanding of the way they can relate to him.

One of the most obvious examples of theology affecting worship is the widespread belief in the necessity of human mediators, a sacerdotal caste of priests whose responsibility is to stand between worshippers and their deity, representing each to the other. Characteristic of the Old Testament, it is unknown in the New. A new principle, the priesthood of all believers, means unhindered access for all worshippers, the only human mediator required being the ascended Jesus at the right hand of his Father in heaven (1 Tim 2:5; Heb 10:19–22; Rev 1:6).

Sadly, the church did not remain consistent with this radical change and soon reverted to the earlier form of priesthood. Even after the Reformation a false distinction was made between 'clergy' and 'laity' (professional and amateur Christians!). Those who were 'ordained' monopolised the preparation and leadership in public acts of worship.

Surprisingly, this pattern persists in many churches that would claim to be 'charismatic' (led by the Spirit) and/or 'evangelical' (based on scripture) – which shows that tradition dies hard. But it is rapidly breaking down and the major reason for its demise has undoubtedly emerged from the charismatic ethos.

Rediscovery of more 'gifts' and therefore more 'ministries' within the body of Christ has dealt a death-blow to the concept of '*the* ministry'. New phrases and slogans have described this recovery of New Testament church life – 'body ministry' and 'every member ministry'. This will and must be expressed in services of worship. Provision must be made by the 'platform' for contributions from the 'floor'. Worship must be more in the hands of the congregation: they should not just be told when and what to say or sing but should also take initiatives of their own.

However, all this is a development across the board and not a difference between charismatic and evangelical worship (one group of the latter, the 'Plymouth Brethren', has advocated this for over a century, though they have often been the most vehemently opposed to 'charismatic' contributions!).

But there is one clear difference between them, which does affect their worship. To begin with outward symptoms, charismatic worship tends to be too casual and evangelical worship tends to be too cerebral. We need to understand the reasons why this is so.

SPONTANEOUS IS NOT SPIRITUAL

A reaction against clericalism often includes retreat from ritualism. Liturgy is associated with priesthood.

Fixed forms of worship are thought to be artificial. There is a desire to be 'natural', to be 'real'. A new objective is introduced: to set people 'free' to worship their Lord. Form is considered the enemy, or at least the inhibitor, of such liberty.

This has led to what can only be described as a 'cultivated informality', illustrated by the fact that it is no longer considered necessary or even helpful to dress more formally to meet with God (though few would do the same for an interview with a potential employer or an introduction to a member of the royal family!). The Bible does, of course, make the point that 'man looks at the outward appearance, but the Lord looks at the heart' (1 Sam 16:7; the context is the selection of a king, not worshippers). This does not, however, make matters of dress or even hairstyle irrelevant (1 Cor 11:3–16; 1 Tim 2:9f). A decline in punctuality is not unrelated to the increase in informality.

But there is a more serious aspect to this relaxed approach

174

to worship. It is the suspicion that the Holy Spirit does not inspire, or even approve of, 'prepared' worship. He prefers to be in direct, immediate control of the worshippers, leading them moment by moment through his 'order of service' rather than theirs. The more spontaneous we can be, the more spiritual we will be.

The results are not encouraging. Often the only preparation is a hasty selection of a few choruses just before the meeting 'to get us going'. The hope presumably is that before these are through, the Spirit will have taken the helm and steer the rest of the service! The predictable programme which usually follows is hardly attributable to the Creator Spirit, since it is usually singularly lacking in creativity.

The truth is that form and freedom need each other and be-long together. Without form there is chaos, without freedom there is death. All attempts to achieve total freedom end up with a new form, often more inflexible than the original rejected one. This has happened already and what might be called the 'charismatic' liturgy is now the same the world over and too familiar to be outlined here.

Its most serious weaknesses are the low level of content and the lack of real progress. Heavily dependent on music, in the shape of repeated 'choruses' accompanied by a 'band' of instrumentalists with electronic amplification, the worship seems calculated to stir the body and spirit without stimulating the mind.

Traditional elements of worship with more didactic content

have been largely abandoned. The reading of scripture has been much reduced, often to those passages immediately relevant to worship (Chapter 5 of Revelation is over-used). Didactic hymns of any length and substance are ignored (this omission is tragic because most ordinary folk learn their doctrine through what they sing). Systematic exposition is squeezed in at the end or abandoned in favour of exhortation. Prayer has been minimised, sometimes limited to a few one-minute bursts between long bouts of singing and rarely including confession or intercession. United confessions of faith (creeds) and responsive prayers are never used.

The lack of real progress in the service is due to the absence of forethought about where the worship is hoped to go and how to get there. But this involves mental definition of strategy and tactics, which can be dismissed as an 'unspiritual' approach. Instead, the general aim seems to be to reach the high point of a charged atmosphere, which is then considered a suitable 'platform of praise' on which a 'word' can be given.

Before considering the positive remedy for these weaknesses, a further one needs to be listed. An overemphasis on 'free expression' can lead to a fragmentation of corporate worship by encouraging a congregation to engage as individuals rather than a body. When a worship leader encourages people to 'do their own thing', to express themselves in the way that feels most comfortable to them ('you can kneel, sit, stand, jump, dance, prostrate yourself – whatever you feel like doing'),

176

the extroverts are quickly separated from the introverts, some doing in public what others would never do even in private. The sense of worshipping together declines and distracting thoughts about each other take attention from the Lord.

The root error, I believe, is the unspoken assumption that the more we prepare worship, the less room for manoeuvre there is for the Holy Spirit. It would be hard to find a scriptural basis for this supposition. Old Testament worshippers had to 'prepare' their sacrifices before they came to the temple and to 'prepare' themselves to meet their God. The fact that our sacrifice is of our own bodies rather than those of animals, praise and thanksgiving rather than fire and smoke, does not mean that we need no preparation.

The alternative to *one* person preparing a complete act of worship is not *no one* preparing (forgive the double negative!) but *everyone* preparing. The 'open' worship of the early church in the homes of the people was not entirely spontaneous. They did not 'ad lib' their way through the service. When they came together each one already had a contribution ready – 'a hymn, or a word of instruction, a revelation, a tongue or an interpretation' (1 Cor 14:26). Nor were the early believers reluctant to use liturgical forms (Acts 2:42 should read '*the* prayers'). Alas, very few congregations come so prepared today, though they could be educated and encouraged to do so.

I believe the Holy Spirit wants to 'conduct' our services in much the same way as a conductor leads an orchestra

177

or choir. In either case it would be a disaster if no one but he had any idea what was going to be played or sung. But that analogy by itself is inadequate since it excludes the spontaneous altogether, unless we picture the conductor taking over one of the instruments and playing it himself. What we really need is a balance between the spontaneous and the prepared. Perhaps the Spirit is most free to release us in worship when we are thoroughly prepared – and willing to abandon all that we have prepared, at his direction. If we can combine the best elements of past forms with the best elements of present freedom, we will achieve a breakthrough in worship. This is being achieved, notably among Catholic charismatic lay people!

Even more important than the place for preparation is the matter of the mind. We should worship with the whole of our being – body, mind and spirit. In concentrating on 'spiritual' adoration, often accompanied by physical expression, charismatic worship has frequently neglected the need of a mental response to the presence of the Almighty, the need to love him with all our mind. Our thoughts need to be stretched, not just our feelings stimulated, in order to 'magnify' the Lord, to get a big enough view of him and offer a big enough 'hallelujah'.

Furthermore, Paul clearly taught that the mind is even more important in corporate worship than in private devotion. Since mutual edification takes precedence over self-expression on such occasions and since mutual edification of each other's spirit is only possible through each other's mind, there must be a constant concern for mental understanding of all that is going on. Intelligibility (which covers hearing and understanding) must characterise every item. This is why Paul was happy to worship with his spirit in private, while his mind was 'unfruitful'; but he did not do so in public. That is why he allowed individual tongues only when they were intelligibly interpreted and forbade corporate tongues altogether. To argue otherwise is childish, not adult, thinking (1 Cor 14:13). Thoughtlessness is infantile.

If charismatics can underemphasise the place of the mind in worship, evangelicals can (and often do) go to the opposite extreme and overemphasise its importance.

MIND IS NOT SPIRIT

Though many evangelicals would look to the Reformation as the second influence on their thinking (after the Bible, of course), they have also been affected by another development from that time, the Renaissance, especially in its later offspring, the Enlightenment, which inaugurated the 'age of reason'. The human mind, with its potential for discovering truth, was exalted to a primary position.

'Rationalism', as it came to be called, had a considerable effect on the thinking of early evangelicals, according to a recent contribution in a collection of essays published as a tribute to John Stott ('Evangelical Christianity and the Enlightenment' in *The Gospel in the Modern World*, Inter-Varsity Press, 1991).

Certainly, there has been an emphasis on the reasonableness of the Christian faith and the importance of instruction in its principles and practice. The sermon has been seen as the climax of worship (the preceding worship has even been called 'the preliminaries'!). Evangelical preaching made few concessions to those not prepared to do some long and hard thinking. An educated ministry systematically enlightened their congregations about the profound truths of biblical revelation.

This partly explains why there is such a strong link with university students and the professions to which they graduated. The evangelical movement has made more headway in middle and upper income groups than among working people. It could be said to be 'intellectually respectable' from one point of view and has captured not a few with outstanding intellectual ability and academic achievement. Until recently, however, it had not produced the kind of biblical scholarship that could withstand the onslaught of the liberal criticism that arose in Germany around the turn of the twentieth century.

Evangelical worship tended to be cerebral. It certainly demanded more activity of the brain than the body! Long prayers and longer sermons required intense mental concentration. The cultivation of right words and thoughts was an important criterion. Hymns were didactic, containing and communicating doctrine to the singers. Everything was planned and prepared (with, perhaps, the exception of extemporary prayer). There was little or no room for spontaneity, especially on the part of the congregation.

The emphasis was on a 'rational' understanding and application of biblical truth. Paul's principle that edification can only be achieved through intelligibility, and therefore the intelligence, was observed to the letter.

We saw (in Chapter 7) that this led to an emphasis on doctrine rather than dynamics, on faith as acceptance rather than action. We must now consider another effect of an overemphasis on the intellect as central to spirituality.

Rationalism rejects the irrational, the illogical, the absurd. Anything is irrational that cannot be explained to human reason. However, since God is God and not man, it is inevitable that he cannot be fully comprehended by mere human reason. His thoughts and ways are higher than ours (Isa 55:8f). Evangelicals, of course, fully accept this and believe that faith goes beyond human reason, but not beyond divine reason. The Creator and his creation are fully 'rational'.

However, while accepting the supra-rational (i.e. above and beyond reason) in the divine realm, evangelicals have traditionally had real reservations about the non-rational in the human realm. Anything that cannot be 'rationalised' (i.e. made sense of to reason) tends to be regarded with suspicion.

To put it another way, evangelicals have real difficulty thinking of the human spirit as a separate entity, able to speak and act on its own without the co-operation of the mind. Mind and spirit are considered so interconnected and interdependent that they can hardly conceive of the spirit by-passing the mind. If it should, then the result can only lead to arbitrary and aimless activity, since the mind is understood as the God-given control of the spirit, to restrain us from irresponsible and excessive behaviour. To activate the spirit without the restraint of the mind would be considered extremely dangerous.

By now the reader will have become aware of the practical implications of this 'rationalistic' line of thinking. The fact is that the spiritual gifts, the *charismata*, fall into the category of the non-rational. They neither use the mind nor are explicable to the mind.

'Tongues' is the clearest example, which may explain why it attracts the most suspicion and even contempt from some evangelicals. While using the gift, the spirit and body are acting without the mind, which remains 'unfruitful', inactive, unproductive (1 Cor 14:14). To evangelicals over-influenced by the Enlightenment, it is incredible that this could possibly be an edifying activity. It appears to them as quite literally 'taking leave of the senses', or at least common sense.

But other word-gifts are equally 'non-sense' and therefore regarded as nonsense. How can anyone speak out a coherent message without the words and sentences first having been formed in the brain? Healing and miracles cannot be 'explained' since the cause cannot be examined, even when the effects are clear.

What, then, do 'rationalistic' evangelicals make of the spiritual gifts?

Some take refuge in a 'dispensational' attitude that limits them to the apostolic period. In this way they can distance themselves from the issue, no longer having to deal with the practical question even if it is not answered in theory. I have been amazed by a kind of schizophrenic attitude to the supernatural among some evangelicals who are entirely credulous towards anything bound between black leather covers and profoundly sceptical about anything like that happening today.

Others 'rationalise' the spiritual gifts until they are so 'normal' that they can be claimed as everyday happenings. One missionary writer claims that the gift of tongues is the ability to learn Japanese in nine months instead of two years; though his colleague, a Reformed theologian, sees it as a harmless, even helpful, psychological safety-valve! In the former case, one wonders why Paul said its use was to edify self rather than evangelise others; in the latter, one wonders why Paul thanked God he had it in such great measure and why he wanted everybody to have it – in a day when psychology was an unknown science.

'Signs following' (Mark 16:16) are interpreted as con-versions after preaching, especially in vestry prayers before a service! 'Prophecy' is said to be 'anointed preaching', though those who make this identification often forbid women to preach, even though Paul assumes they will prophesy (1 Cor 11:5). 'Wisdom' and 'knowledge' are the fruits of long experience and deep study; this interpretation ignores the fact that the gifts are 'a *word* of wisdom' and 'a *word* of knowledge' and therefore brief utterances (1 Cor 12:8).

And so it goes on, a 'demythologising' process that boils down the dynamic 'spiritual' gifts into dedicated 'natural' gifts, with which we are more familiar. The tragic effect of this is to limit leadership and ministry to those who are most naturally gifted, and therefore to those who have 'got on in the world' and had more opportunities to do so. Inevitably, the membership will then reflect the leadership and the church will be locked into one social stratum.

One thing that is clear from scripture is that this is not God's way. He delights to give spiritual gifts to those who are not naturally gifted. He loves to use the 'nobodies' to confound the 'somebodies'. Jesus built his church with fishermen, tax clerks and tentmakers. This way, the Lord gets the glory.

It is not a coincidence that the amazing growth of pentecostal churches in the twentieth century has been among the poorer and less educated masses, particularly in the so-called 'third world', actually the 'two-thirds' world. The 'non-rational' can touch their spirits.

* * * * *

Before leaving the subject of worship, I have a radical suggestion to make which I believe would help both charismatics and evangelicals to move in the right direction and towards each other.

That is to *reverse the normal order of service* in both streams and minister the word to people before ministering to the Lord in worship.

There is nothing new in this, though it will come as a surprise, even a shock, to those who have never known anything other than the familiar pattern and didn't know there was ever anything else.

It was the universal practice in the early church, according to all the records we have. There is a full account in an early document called the *Didache*. The Christians met for two hours 'on the day of the sun'. The first hour was spent in the reading and explanation of the scriptures, the second in worship, culminating at the Lord's table (i.e. communion).

This order was not original. It was simply taken over from Jewish practice, which has survived to this day, as a visit to any synagogue on Saturday morning will confirm. It was therefore the form familiar to Jesus and the apostles; they saw no reason to change it.

There is something very appropriate about listening to God before addressing him. Worship is, after all, a response to what he has done for us and said to us, an expression of gratitude for his grace.

Instead of worship being regarded as a preparation for the word, the word is seen as a preparation for worship, which becomes the real climax. And there are obvious practical advantages.

For one thing, few congregations are ready to worship as soon as they arrive, as many of those responsible for leading worship know only too well. People begin to worship when they are more conscious of the Lord than of themselves or each other; it can take twenty minutes or more to reach this stage. But after hearing the word, their minds are so full of the Lord that they are ready to worship. Alas, so often at this point, when they need to express their response, there is only time for a final song and benediction.

For another, the word will give content and variety to the worship, as a response to what has been heard. Praise and prayer will be related to the message and to each other. The mood will vary, depending on what has been received. Sometimes it will be loud and exuberant, rejoicing in God's goodness; at other times it will be quiet and reverent, in awe of his holiness.

The twenty minutes or so saved at the beginning can now be given to spontaneous contributions or personal ministry at the end. Taking bread and wine together is a fitting conclusion, instead of being squeezed in between worship and sermon.

Even the word is less likely to be forgotten by remaining in the context of worship than by rushing home to a meal.

Of course, it makes more demand on the teacher (some could kill worship dead!); the word must be living and active. And on the worship leader, who can be adjusting his prepared items, even changing them, as he senses the response of the people to the word (he should sit where he can see their faces).

Such a change could combine the strengths of charismatic and evangelical worship and overcome some of their weaknesses.

12

HOLINESS

Spiritual gifts do not in themselves divide Christians from one another; but attitudes towards them do, both in those who have them and those who don't. Their appearance within a fellowship can signal a crisis, for the presence or absence of love will be quickly revealed. Without love, feelings of superiority in some and inferiority in others soon cause cracks in the edifice.

Years ago I lived in a village which had an ambitious football team. A wealthy supporter gave them a large cheque to buy new clothing and equipment. But the players argued so much about how it should be spent, even about the new colours on their jerseys, that the team eventually broke up and ceased to play. The donor must have regretted his generosity, though his gift was only the occasion and not the cause of the rift and therefore he was not to blame for what happened. Readers can draw their own conclusion and make their own application.

Power is always dangerous in the wrong hands. To be baptised in Spirit is to receive power (Luke 24:49; Acts 1:8). The gifts that this releases can do great good – and great harm. Everything depends on the character of those who exercise them.

Both charismatics and evangelicals need to understand the biblical relationship between spiritual gifts and holiness or, rather, the lack of it. Both need to realise that there is no inevitable progress from one to the other.

GIFTS ARE NOT FRUIT

One reason for the appeal of spiritual gifts is their immediate availability. Just as soon as the Spirit has been received, any one of these supernatural abilities can also be given.

The fact is that God has chosen not to wait until a believer is mature, much less perfect, before equipping them for his service. Had he decided to do so, there would be a noticeable shortage of gifts around; and the few who had them could legitimately assume they were superior to others without them. But the situation is precisely the opposite: the gifts have been generously and widely distributed and in no way indicate that their possessors are better than others.

A profound theological principle lies behind this divine

largesse. Christianity is the only religion in the world which puts justification before sanctification. In all others, adherents have to perfect themselves before being accepted; in ours God accepts us as we are in order to help us become what we ought to be. We are justified by faith, not works. And we are justified in order to be sanctified. All this is grace, which is undeserved generosity.

Both the gift of the Spirit and the spiritual gifts are examples of this grace; the latter are called *charismata* in Greek, derived from *charis*, the word for grace. I like to hear them called 'grace-gifts', as Catholic charismatics do. They are examples of his mercy, not our merit. They are a proof of our justification, but not of our sanctification. They are the badge of a sinner who has received grace, not a saint (except in title; God calls us 'saints' or 'holy ones' even before we have begun to live up to such a description, Rom 1:7; 2 Cor 1:1; Eph 1:1; 'called to be saints' is a mistranslation for the words 'to be' are not in the original text).

All this is easily forgotten. Power can be intoxicating. Since supernatural power is superior to natural, those who possess supernatural gifts easily feel superior to those whose service relies only on natural gifts, which are often considerably less spectacular. There is a sense of having reached a higher plane of achievement, of having 'arrived' among the spiritual elite.

It is a delusion and a dangerous one. Nothing could be further from the truth. The reality is that gifts are in no way indicative of quality of character and are not status symbols at all. It is possible for them to be exercised in carnality, by 'fleshly' people in 'fleshly' ways. Samson is a 'good' example from the Old Testament; the whole Corinthian church from the New. The latter had all the spiritual gifts, yet needed both moral and doctrinal correction. We owe Paul's matchless 'Hymn of Love' to their immaturity (1 Cor 13; though it should really be entitled 'Gifts Without Love' – see Appendix B). The church was in disorder, division and even disgrace (drunkenness at the Lord's table!). In such a context the exercise of gifts breaks down rather than builds up the fellowship.

Charismatics need to be constantly reminded of the need to grow and mature, the need to 'go on being filled with Spirit' (Eph 5:18). Maturity comes from *walking* in the Spirit, not clapping, jumping or dancing in the Spirit! Walking is better exercise, even if it is less exciting! It involves taking one step at a time in the direction the Spirit leads.

Those who continue to walk in this 'way' will produce the fruit of the Spirit. The works of the flesh are plural and can appear separately; the fruit of the Spirit is singular and all nine 'flavours' appear together. Three relate us to God (love, joy, peace), three to others (patience, kindness, goodness) and three to ourselves (faithfulness, meekness, self-control). No unbeliever has more than a few of these characteristics. Only one person displayed them all in full measure and perfect balance: the Lord Jesus himself. In producing this fruit, the

Spirit of Christ within us is seeking to reproduce his character. But all fruit takes time to grow, mature and ripen; by contrast, both the works of the flesh and the gifts of the Spirit can appear instantaneously, though never simultaneously (Gal 5:16f). They are direct products of the flesh and Spirit already present in the believer; fruit is the indirect by-product of putting the flesh to death and living in the Spirit.

Maturity consists in exercising the gifts with the fruit, especially in love. This is the 'more excellent way' advocated by Paul (1 Cor 12:31; 14:1). Every charismatic should have this ambition and the constant consciousness of falling short will keep him or her humble!

To have been 'filled' is not necessarily to be 'full'. Since evangelicals are just as confused, if not more, on this point, we shall develop it in the next section. The New Testament clearly distinguishes between those who have been 'filled' once and those who are 'full' continually; the first was true of all disciples in those days, the second of only some. To mistake one for the other fosters the illusion of having arrived rather than just set out. The term 'Spirit-filled Christian' fails to make this distinction and perpetuates the confusion.

Finally, there are two 'negative' truths which we do well to remember.

First, spiritual gifts *can be taken away*. God is incredibly patient, but his patience can be exhausted. This is not a weakness in his character, but the reaction of his holiness to wilful persistence in unholy behaviour. Again, Samson is an obvious and outstanding example. His tragic story illustrates the danger of assuming that past anointings and achievements in the power of the Spirit bring immunity from divine judgement (Jud 16:20). Not all those who have done mighty works in the Lord's name will be recognised by him at the last (Matt 7:21–23). It is possible for those who have 'tasted the powers of the age to come', to 'fall away'; and for such there is no possibility of finding their way back (Heb 6:4–6). Such sober warnings should stimulate us to press on toward the goal to win the prize for which we have been called (Phil 3:14).

Second, spiritual gifts *will pass away*. They are very necessary to build up the church, but they are the scaffolding rather than the building itself. They are the means, not the end. One day, when the edifice is complete, they will all become obsolete. What need will there be of the gift of healing when we all have new resurrection bodies? What need of tongues when we all enjoy perfect communion and therefore communication with God (as Jesus did, which may explain why this is the one gift he is never recorded to have used)? What need of a word of knowledge, when we know God (and others) as well as he now knows us? To focus our ambitions on gifts or, even sadder, to find our identity or security in them is to rely on the temporal (and temporary) rather than the eternal (and permanent).

When the gifts disappear, what will remain? Faith, hope and love, that trinity of Christian virtues which figures so prominently in the New Testament (1 Cor 13:13; 1 Thess 4:8; 1 Pet 1:3, 5, 8). Faith relates to all that God has done in the past, hope to all that he has promised to do in the future, but love makes him real in the present. Even among these three lasting qualities, one stands supreme. That is because it is the very nature of God (1 John 4:7–16).

Spiritual gifts, then, have their place and an important role to play. But they are temporary and their importance must not be exaggerated. In the last analysis what we *are* is far more significant than what we *do*. The Spirit is the Holy Spirit and far more concerned that we share the divine character than divine capabilities, his purity than his power. Heavenly love is both the vital ingredient and the ultimate objective in all charismatic activity.

FILLED IS NOT FULL

We have already noted a tendency among evangelicals, especially those who are 'anti-charismatic', to use static nouns rather than dynamic verbs when describing the work of the Holy Spirit. They talk about 'the baptism and fullness' of the Spirit. This gives the impression of an impersonal package rather than a personal encounter. But there are more serious implications hidden in such usage. It leads to an unbiblical distinction and an unbiblical identification, both of which have profound practical consequences.

The use of nouns makes possible a separation of 'baptism' and 'fullness'; the former is associated with justification and the beginning of the Christian life, the latter with sanctification and its end. This creates a gulf between them, chronologically as well as theologically. It is then extremely unlikely, if not impossible, for anyone to receive both at the same time. Yet the New Testament describes Pentecost with both verbs, 'baptised' and 'filled' (Acts 1:5; 2:4). Even more significant, this event was never directly linked with either the justification or sanctification of those concerned. The data simply does not fit this distinction.

The use of the noun 'fullness' has also made possible an identification of the verb 'filled' and the adjective 'full'. The concept is then completely separated from initiation and totally associated with the process of maturation, particularly its culmination.

This breeds an extreme reluctance to testify to having been 'filled' and critical suspicion of those who do so. It is 'heard' as a claim to perfection or at least a high degree of sanctification. This is then considered a self-contradicting testimony, at worst arrogance and at best presumption. To say one has been 'filled with the (Holy) Spirit' is taken to mean one is 'full of (the Spirit of) holiness'.

When this fused meaning is used by evangelicals to appraise charismatics, a negative judgement is almost inevitable. They are certainly not all 'full of holiness'. They are often 'baby' and even 'carnal' Christians, as the Corinthians were. The reality of their experience is seriously questioned: 'How can they possibly have been filled with the *Holy* Spirit when their lives reveal so little holiness?' Scepticism is then extended to the gifts they claim to have: 'How could the *Holy* Spirit give gifts to such immature people?'

This critical approach is prone to draw unfavourable comparison with saintly evangelicals who are 'non-charismatic'. It is easy to find them and to demonstrate the contrast. Many are far more wise, loving and dedicated in their use of natural gifts than those with spiritual gifts. And they often demonstrate grace in conduct, conversation and character that can put some enthusiastic charismatics to shame.

But is this a fair, or even an accurate, comparison? To contrast a mature evangelical with an immature charismatic can be as misleading as the common comparison between the best people outside church and the worst inside!

Scripture discourages us from comparing ourselves with others or others with ourselves. The Lord is not impressed with 'I thank you that I am not like others'; even 'There, but for the grace of God, go I' could be similarly motivated.

Scripture encourages us to compare ourselves as we are with ourselves as we could be, if we allowed the Spirit to do all he wants to do with us. The right judgements are: 'How much more attractive this gifted charismatic would be if he had the fruit as well!' and, 'How much more effective this gracious evangelical would be if he had the gifts as well!'

This would avoid the false antithesis suggested by: 'Which would you rather have in your church, the gifts or the fruit?' That's like being asked: 'Would you rather have bread or butter with your cup of tea?'

If gifts without fruit are inadequate, fruit without gifts is ineffective. A 'fruity' Christian has a sick friend in hospital. He shows love by visiting him, peace by calming his fears, joy by cheering him up, patience by listening to a detailed account of his surgery, kindness by removing his bedpan, goodness by giving him a bunch of grapes, faithfulness by visiting him every day, meekness by leaving promptly when the nurse says visiting hours are over and self-control by not eating the grapes! But he has left him sick. The fruit of the Spirit cannot cure anyone; healing is a gift of the Spirit.

So let us announce a moratorium on all false contrasts and comparisons. Let us acknowledge that gifts and fruit belong together, Spirit and scripture belong together, charismatics and evangelicals belong together.

But we haven't quite finished with this matter. Behind a false comparison lies faulty thinking. Earlier it was claimed that the use of the unbiblical noun 'fullness' to describe the work of the Spirit was misleading because it fused 'filled' and 'full' into one word and therefore one concept, tying both to sanctification, to the later, mature phase of the Christian life – and therefore denying the possibility of being 'filled' at an earlier, immature stage. The 'filling' comes at the end rather than the beginning, an effect of progress rather than its cause, a reward rather than a foretaste, a goal rather than a goad. Is this biblical thinking?

The New Testament seems to link 'filled' with initiation and justification, 'full' with maturation and sanctification. 'Filled' is synonymous with other phrases and words like 'received', 'baptised', 'sealed', 'anointed', 'fallen upon', 'poured out', all of which are used to describe the *beginning* of life in the Spirit. However, alone among them, 'filled' is also used to describe later conscious and dynamic encounters with the Holy Spirit (cf Acts 2:4 with 4:31). So, while one is 'baptised' in Spirit only once, it is possible to be 'filled' again and again. The verb can be repeated. All the believers in the early church had been 'filled' once and some more than once.

The adjective 'full' is used quite differently and more selectively. It is a necessary qualification for special responsibility; it applies to those with a high reputation among the saints, who are 'known to be full of Holy Spirit' (Acts 6:3). In the same passage some associated qualities are mentioned: full of wisdom, full of faith, full of grace, full of power (Acts 6:3, 5, 8). Spiritual maturity is clearly indicated. It is significant that Stephen, to whom these outstanding attributes are primarily applied, is still said to be 'full of Holy Spirit' in the very last moments of his life, as he became the first martyr for the faith (Acts 7:55).

How can we conceive ourselves and communicate to others this distinction between 'filled' and 'full'? How can anyone, or anything for that matter, be filled without becoming full?

I use a simple illustration from the kitchen, which doesn't prove anything but seems to clarify a lot. Some uncooked potatoes are put in a saucepan, which is then held under a running tap to 'fill' it with water. It is rapidly filled to overflowing, which is immediately apparent. But it would be inaccurate to say that this is now a saucepan 'full' of water; indeed, the amount of water could be comparatively small, certainly much less than the empty saucepan could hold. In order for it to become 'full' of water, two things have to happen. Negatively, the potatoes must be removed; positively, the tap must be kept turned on, so that the water continues to flow and fill the space left by the potatoes. It is a simple analogy but one, I believe, which conveys the true scriptural significance of 'filled' and 'full'.

For a person to be 'full' of Holy Spirit, the desires of the flesh have to be removed and the filling of the Spirit must be continued. Was it not D.L. Moody who, when asked if he had been filled with the Spirit, replied: 'Yes, but I leak'?

In other words, we need to be more careful with our words. To stray from biblical terminology can lead us away from biblical theology. We then have misconceptions about ourselves and others. Charismatics have been mistaken in thinking that because they have been filled they must be full. Evangelicals have been mistaken in thinking that it is impossible to be filled without becoming full. Both *can* be 'filled' to overflowing right away and both must press on toward becoming 'full'.

Which leaves one question: what is the relation, if any, between 'filled' and 'full'? To put it in its starkest form, can anyone become 'full' without first having been 'filled'?

If 'baptism in Spirit' is a 'second blessing' or even a second 'reception' and is only an influx of power for service, the question need not be asked. There is no necessary connection between the two. Salvation, and therefore sanctification, springs from the first blessing or reception. To be 'filled' is not essential to being 'full'.

If, however, as has been argued in these pages, there is only one 'reception' of the Spirit for salvation *and* service, which is the same as being 'baptised in' and 'filled with' Holy Spirit, then there must be a connection. To be filled is a necessary step towards being 'full'.

How can this question be settled? For some it is simply a matter of experience – 'I've known many saintly people who have never had what you call the experience of being filled.' Actually, it can't be settled as easily as that. For one thing, what we mean by 'saintly' may not be the same as the apostolic understanding of 'full'; remember that in Stephen's case it meant being full of power as well as grace (Acts 6:8). For another, closer investigation of the lives of many saints reveals that they have experienced such a 'filling' at some time in their lives but were reluctant to talk about it for fear of being thought to be claiming to be 'full'. In any case, such questions must be answered from scripture rather than experience, especially by those calling themselves evangelicals.

Here we run into a difficulty. In one sense, the New Testament does not, indeed cannot, give us an answer – because the question never arose. Since every single believer in those days had been 'filled', they knew of no single case of a person who was 'full' without having first been filled. It was taken for granted that the one led to the other and made it possible. They would probably have been astonished by any suggestion of having one without the other. How could anyone 'go on being filled' if they had not already been filled? How could anyone be 'full' of the Holy Spirit without having first 'received' him?

The answer to our question may be that it should never have been asked! When we recognise that it is only asked because we have introduced people to Jesus and to his Father through him but failed to introduce them to the Spirit, we shall humbly seek to recover the full apostolic understanding and practice of Christian initiation (see Chapter 9 and my book: *The Normal Christian Birth*).

Meanwhile, we are free to explore the ways in which having been 'filled' is of help to becoming 'full'.

What an incentive it is to have received an earnest, a foretaste, the first down-payment (all this is included in the Greek word *arrabon*). This initial instalment simply whets the appetite for more.

As well as giving an incentive, being filled increases belief in the possibility of becoming full. The experience convinces the recipient that God is able to do anything he wishes with a life totally surrendered into his hands.

There will also now be a conscious familiarity with the dynamic that will achieve the 'fullness'. The power has been made available.

Above all, there will now be a genuinely personal relationship with the Holy Spirit which makes the immanence of God an existential fact. While Father and Son are in heaven, the Spirit has not only taken the latter's place on earth but is God-in-us and not just 'God-with-us' (*immanu-el*, the immanent God). This is just one reason why it is even 'better' to have the third than the second person of the Trinity here on earth (John 16:7).

It would be utterly foolish to claim that there is more 'holiness' among charismatics than evangelicals, or vice-versa! It would be difficult, if not impossible, to engage in adequate research to reach such a conclusion, or even to decide on the criteria to be used. It is extremely doubtful if such a comparison is even valid.

The real question is: what would be the effect on our sanctification of the total integration of these two streams? That can only be answered after it has happened. Since the first century we have not had the opportunity to observe a church in which every member has been 'filled' and from that foundation is eagerly pursuing the objective of being 'full'. Will our generation enable the world to see the result and stand amazed at the mightiest miracle of all – to change human nature?

There will come a day when every member of the church will be 'full' as well as 'filled', when the goal will be reached; but that belongs to the future. That wonderful state awaits the second advent of our Lord Jesus Christ; but the certainty of it is one of the strongest motives for anticipating it as much as possible here and now (1 John 3:2f). Even so, come, Lord Jesus!

EPILOGUE

EPILOGUE:
THE JOINED STICKS

The kingdom of Israel was only united for a very brief period— the three reigns of Saul, David and Solomon. The last had much wisdom for others but little for himself (a common failing!). His extravagance was just one of the factors that led to the civil war after his death. It was the beginning of a tragic decline in the moral and spiritual life of the nation which disqualified her from occupying the promised land.

The ten tribes of 'Israel' in the north were the first to go, deported by the Assyrians. The two tribes of 'Judah' in the south followed, when Jerusalem was destroyed by the Babylonians. Their exile was shared by a priestly prophet called 'God's strong man' (in Hebrew 'Ezekiel').

His vision of a resurrected nation, in the 'valley of dry bones', is one of the most famous in the whole Bible, having provided inspiration for many sermons and not a few songs. However, in the same chapter (37) of his book is another, equally important yet hardly known.

Ezekiel was told to find two sticks, write 'Ephraim', representing the ten northern tribes, on one and 'Judah', representing the two southern tribes, on the other. He was then to hold them together in his hand and they would fuse together into one. Whether this was seen in vision or was an actual physical event, a miracle, is not clear, though the language favours the latter (which is no more incredible than Moses' rod becoming a snake).

The symbolic meaning is not ambiguous. As the two sticks became one in Ezekiel's hand, so the two parts of his people, separated for centuries, would again be united in God's hand. There would only be one king ('my servant David'). God would make an everlasting covenant of peace with this united people, establishing them and increasing their numbers. And the ultimate purpose was that 'the nations will know' (a favourite phrase of Ezekiel's) that God makes people whole.

Some years ago, a picture came into my mind (I put it no stronger than that). I saw two sticks, but in this case they were held in two hands and held together end to end. On one was written 'charismatic' and on the other 'evangelical'. They fused together; one hand let go and the other brandished the enlarged stick as a weapon, far more effective than either of the two shorter ones would have been.

This book was born in that moment. Encouraged by this 'vision' I began to speak about it at seminars for church leaders, both in this country and overseas. As so often when teaching others, I educated myself. I saw more and more clearly the differences that remained and how they could be resolved.

The response was positive. Mutual suspicion gave way to mutual understanding, if not immediate agreement. Instead of seeing only the errors of the other, each side began to look again at possible mistakes of their own. Instead of my material being rejected as much too negative and critical (as I had both thought it was and expected it to be perceived by others), it was accepted and even welcomed as a breakthrough. Of course, that was in its verbal form when vocal tone and facial expression make it much easier to sense the spirit in which things are said than may be the case with cold print.

These 'live' occasions enabled me to gauge reactions and discover the kind of questions raised in the hearers' minds by my basic thesis; many of these, and my attempted answers, are incorporated in this book. There is one, however, which came up frequently and which I feel I ought to deal with here.

I was often asked why I limited my concern to these two streams. What about the others, who would not identify themselves with either? In particular, the 'Catholic' stream was often cited, though by charismatic rather than evangelical questioners! Ever since Bishop Lesslie Newbigin's prophetic plea to include the 'third force' of pentecostalism in ecumenical thinking, along with the Catholic and evangelical (in *The Household of God*, SCM, 1953), many have adopted this tripartite analysis of church life. However, one could extend the subdivision indefinitely. There is a large segment who would use the description 'liberal', rather than any of the three.

There are reasons why my thinking, speaking and now writing have been confined to two. It is not just that my original 'vision' was limited in this way, nor that these two are those of which I have most personal experience and knowledge; though I admit these subjective factors played their part. There were objective reasons. These two are not only the *fastest* growing branches of the church; they could be said to be the *only* ones that are growing. I sincerely believe that the future of the church in the next millennium, if the Lord does not return soon, belongs to them.

This is not to say that other strands should be ignored. They have a contribution to make. We can learn from them all, both positively from their strengths and negatively from their weaknesses; and must be open to do so. But they are all, for different reasons, in serious decline.

One of the main reasons for 'catholic' recession is persistence in dividing priesthood and people, clergy and laity—which belongs to the old covenant rather than the new. Professional monopoly inhibits the Spirit's activity. Charismatic and evangelical infiltration have been largely at lay level and have been carefully controlled by the hierarchy.

The 'liberals' have accomplished their own downfall by robbing themselves of the power of the gospel to save those who believe. Scepticism over the supernatural dimensions of scripture has left them with a message little different from the best humanists. It is difficult to retain the spiritual when the supernatural has been discarded.

So the horizons of this study have been deliberately limited. I trust this will be understood and not prove unnecessarily offensive. In any case, it is unlikely that it will be read by many outside the circles for which it is intended.

I conclude with two pleas, one 'internal' and the other 'external'. Both prompt the question: can we afford not to be integrated? The union of charismatics and evangelicals is not just desirable, it is imperative – both for their own sakes and the sake of others.

How much they need each other! The reader must have noticed how often the dual critiques in Part II have matched and complemented each other. One needs more theology with their experience; the other needs more experience with their theology. One needs more scripture with their prophecies; the other needs more prophecies with their scripture. One needs less emphasis on tongues; the other needs more. One needs to use the mind as well as the spirit; the other needs to exercise the spirit as well as the mind.

How will these imbalances be corrected – separately or together? It is obvious that each needs what the other has, but will they try and get it by themselves or from each other?

It would be easier, as well as more edifying for the whole body, if we got together to get it together! It may even be that the head of the church will not allow us to have all that we need without each other. Unity is very dear to his heart, as is truth (John 17:17–21).

So with a humble and teachable spirit we need to reach out to each other. The final stages of integration will not be without heart-searching pain. The pace of progress will not be uniform. But the prize will be worth it, not just for ourselves, but for many others.

Just as Ezekiel's vision promised an increase in numbers to God's reunited people, we can expect the same to result from this reintegration of the New Testament people of God.

Statistical studies have demonstrated the spectacular growth that becomes possible. One study among Baptists in England (by the Bible Society in 1981) showed that whereas 'evangelical' churches were growing at an average of around five per cent per annum, the rate for 'charismatic evangelical' churches was twenty-five per cent. Who would not want to see their effectiveness multiplied five-fold?

In other words, it is for the sake of the world, and not just the church, that we need to combine forces. It is ultimately for the lost that we need to sanctify ourselves for the task of uniting our two streams.

God's purpose in giving us his Spirit and the scripture was that we might be equipped to bring the good news of salvation to a sad and sinful society that does not know why it is here or where it is going. That is why he needs a people who are both charismatic and evangelical.

APPENDICES

APPENDIX A

WHY DID PAUL WRITE
TO THE ROMANS?

How significant is it that charismatic distinctives are missing from this epistle? Our answer will depend on what we think was Paul's reason for writing it. If he was summarising the essential elements of the Christian gospel and its application to life, this omission would indicate their relative unimportance. If he was primarily dealing with the needs of his readers (as in all his other letters), the silence simply indicates that they were not having problems in this area. It would be no more an indication of his evaluation than the total absence of any reference to the central act of Christian worship (taking bread and wine in remembrance of Christ's death). The correspondence with the Corinthians makes an interesting comparison.

So why did Paul write to the Romans?

In the absence of a cheap, rapid and reliable mail service

in the ancient world, there had to be a very good reason for writing a letter, especially since someone had to be found to deliver it.

Because of the expense involved, most were quite short, up to two hundred words; though Cicero managed one of two-and-a-half thousand, while Seneca topped four thousand (about the length of each chapter in Part II of this volume). Paul averaged thirteen hundred. The fact that his letter to the Romans is the longest surviving letter, both in the New Testament and outside it, surpassing seven thousand words, is just one of the features that make it unique and worthy of special attention.

It is unusual for other reasons. There are far more opening and closing greetings. It reads more like a lecture than a letter, the style is more appropriate to a spoken than a written message, as if it has been transcribed rather than dictated, with dialogue as well as monologue.

The tone and temperature are cooler than usual for him. Many of his letters are highly charged with emotion: he scolds, cajoles, pleads. This one is more intellectual, less subjective and more objective.

Normally, the first clue to understanding apostolic correspondence is to identify the situation to which it corresponds. In other words, it is necessary to reconstruct the need of the readers to receive the letter, by reading the lines and between the lines. Why did the letter have to be written?

This detection is much easier with the letters to Corinth and

Galatia than this one to Rome. There is no mention of crisis or controversy requiring correction, no 'scent of battle'. The first impression is that it could have been written anywhere, any time – more like a published book than a directed letter, or at least a circular letter that could be passed on to other churches as well.

One obvious reason for these differences from his other correspondence is that this letter alone is written to a church that Paul did not start and had not seen. It is written before he has had any personal relationship with the fellowship, though he has met some members elsewhere. His knowledge of their circumstances is indirect, second-hand. So it is understandable that his tone is not that used when addressing his spiritual children, the churches he himself has planted.

But why did he write at all? As he says in the letter, he has no desire to 'build on someone else's foundation' (Rom 15:20). The problem is compounded by the fact that no specific purpose is stated; it can only be deduced or inferred from its contents.

Scholars have produced at least a dozen hypotheses! But most have agreed that the reason is to be sought in the writer rather than the reader, though this would be contrary to all his other letters. They have posed themselves the question: 'why did Paul need to write it?' Their answers can be grouped under two main suggestions. Both are based on his situation when he wrote.

The year is AD 55. Paul has been preaching for twenty

years and has completed his mission in the eastern Mediterranean basin. That is, he has planted a self-supporting, self-governing, self-propagating colony of the kingdom in the major centre of population in each region or province, leaving them to evangelise the rest. His final task among them is to make a collection for the poor brethren in Jerusalem and take it there himself. He is pausing in Greece for three months before making the journey. He has time to write, time to get these spoken words into written form, leaving a permanent record of his 'gospel'.

So here are his mature reflections, his last will and testament. Not knowing how much longer he can travel and speak, he composes his 'manifesto'. It is a summary of what he has preached, hence its feel of a 'lecture', or a circular letter.

The 'dialogue' is explained by the fact that he used this method to communicate the gospel (the word *dialegomai* is actually used of him, as it was frequently of Jesus). He has argued and been heckled (Acts 17:2, 17; 18:4, 19; 19:8, 9; 24:25). He knows all the objections; he now has all the answers. This explains the high incidence of rhetorical questions (e.g. Rom 4:1; 6:1, 15; etc.).

But why should he then send this record of his preaching to Rome? Some say it was because Rome was the *capital of the empire*. The apostle to the Gentiles must surely have wanted to take his gospel to the imperial centre of the Gentile world, having taken it to the provincial centres. In case he is prevented from coming in person, he sends his gospel in advance, in the form of an epistle, though not with the usual content. In a word, Paul's 'need' was to fulfil an ambition to reach Rome.

Others find the clue in his ambition to reach beyond Rome. This theory sees Rome as the *gateway to the west*. As Antioch has served as his base in the east, Paul is now seeking a new base for the west, since Antioch would be too distant. So Paul only plans to visit, not to stay and certainly not to 'take over' leadership. He hopes to have their support in his ongoing mission; it is unlikely that he refers to finance, since he never received or expected this from Antioch or anywhere else.

Why should he recount his 'gospel' in order to raise support? The usual theory is that he is submitting it for their approval. They may well have heard rumours that he was a controversial and even heretical preacher (fostered by his 'Judaising' opponents, who did not think he gave adequate attention to the law of Moses). So to gain the Romans' confidence, he laid out his theology before them, to demonstrate his orthodoxy.

Such is the usual explanation, with variations, as to how this letter came to be written. Notice that it is based on the needs of the writer rather than the readers, which is so unusual, even unique for Paul, that it may and must be questioned, especially if the more usual reason can be found.

While there are no doubt elements of truth in this approach, which may have played a minor role in eliciting the letter, there are serious doubts as to whether it provides the major reason.

First, Paul's plans for the west are mentioned (15:24), but in a 'newsy' section at the end, which is a highly unusual position for the main purpose of a letter.

Second, Paul was not given to seeking human approval for his message. Having claimed to receive it direct from the risen, ascended Lord, he neither sought nor needed approval, even from the other apostles (see Galatians 1:11–2:10). This would be the first time in his career he had sought such authorisation; he avoided 'letters of commendation' (2 Cor 3:1).

Third, it is assumed that Paul is writing to get something from his readers, whereas his declared desire is to impart something to them (Rom 1:11). His primary ambition is to minister to them; support for his ministry is quite secondary.

Fourth, this hypothesis offers no explanation for half the letter (chapters 9–16). Chapters 9–11 are invariably regarded as a self-contained parenthesis on a 'pet' theme of Paul's and not an integral part of his 'gospel'. But we need to remember that Paul did not divide his letters into chapters (it is a tragedy that they later were); and if these divisions are removed, there is a clear continuity from 8 to 9 ('who shall separate us from a God who is for us? . . . what about the Jews?') and from 11 to 12 ('that he may have mercy on all . . . I beseech you, by the mercies of God'). Nor do chapters 12–15 present an adequate summary of Paul's ethical teaching; they deal only with a few specific issues of relationships – with enemies, with state officials and, most of all, with fellow-believers.

Fifth, and this is the most significant criticism for our purpose, even chapters 1–8 do not provide a comprehensive account of the 'gospel' Paul preached, though the opposite is almost universally assumed! Some central themes are missing. We know from the book of Acts that the 'kingdom' of God was fundamental to Paul's message (Acts 14:22; 19:8; 28:23, 31). Yet the word occurs only once in Romans and then in the wrong section (14:17)!

The eschatological (that which pertains to the 'end', the *eschaton*, of history) is missing. Apart from a passing reference to the Day of Judgement, there is no emphasis on the Second Coming of Christ (which, judging by his correspondence with Thessalonica, was a major theme with Paul). The fatherhood of God and the divinity of Christ are muted; they are certainly not prominent. The 'church' is never mentioned.

Other themes seem to occupy an inordinate amount of space. Justification completely overshadows other aspects of initiation such as repentance and regeneration. Abraham is given extraordinary prominence – a whole chapter to himself!

It is a mistake, therefore, to take chapters 1–8 as a precis of Paul's preaching, as embodying his 'gospel', much less as his 'systematic theology'. As with his ethical section, chapters 12–16, we have a careful selection of, and special emphasis on, certain themes particularly relevant to his purpose in writing.

But what was that purpose? Since the reason for writing all his other letters is found in his readers, there is a possibility, even a probability, that this is also the case here. At least, this should be explored first, before looking elsewhere.

Can such a reason be found within the church at Rome? Remember that we are looking for an explanation of the whole letter, chapters 9–11 and 12–16, as well as 1–8. Is there any need in the readers that ties all three sections together and explains both the emphases and omissions in each of them?

When put this way, a clear answer to the question emerges. The clues lie in the peculiar history of this metropolitan and cosmopolitan fellowship.

Neither Peter nor Paul established this church, though both were later associated with it. No one knows who started it, but there were 'Jews and proselytes' from Rome listening to Peter's preaching on the day of Pentecost (Acts 2:10f). If these laid the foundation, as seems extremely likely, it was largely composed at first of Jewish believers, as in many other places.

Many of their early converts would be from the synagogues; there was a Hebrew colony of forty thousand in that city. But it would not be long before Gentile converts, from the city and elsewhere, would join the church, especially since 'all roads led to Rome'.

Then the Emperor Claudius banished all Jews from Rome. The trouble apparently arose over one called 'Chrestus', which may refer to Christ, and could indicate the common experience of internecine strife over those 'converting' to the Christian faith (which had dogged Paul's ministry). Among those expelled at that time were Aquila and Priscilla, who were tent makers and met up with Paul in Corinth (Acts 18:2). So the church in Rome became wholly Gentile, in leadership and membership.

Claudius died a few years later (in AD 54) and was succeeded by Nero, who in his earlier years listened to advice and exercised a more tolerant reign than he did later. The Jews were allowed to return and flooded back. But the believers among them found it far from easy to reintegrate into the church. By now Gentiles were in the majority and in control. The 'quantity' of later Gentile believers was threatened by the reappearance of 'quality' early Jewish believers. The former were claiming, with some arrogance, that it was inevitable that Gentiles should take over from Jews, who had as a race rejected Christ (this was the first example of 'replacement' theology: the teaching that Israel is finished because her place has been taken by the church as the 'new Israel').

This tension was building up to a crisis. News of it reached Paul. Someone was desperately needed to avert a disaster. At worst, the church could be destroyed; at best, it would be divided into two 'denominations', which could spread throughout the empire. Yet Paul was not free to visit them straight away and by the time he could reach them it would probably be too late. But he could and did write a letter, just months after the Jewish return to Rome (which cannot be a coincidence).

He was uniquely qualified to handle the problem, combining as he did an upbringing as a Jew (and a Roman citizen) with a calling to the Gentiles. But he was handicapped by the fact that he was not personally known to them, had not been their 'founding father' and, above all, had not been invited to sort out their problems. He could hardly chide them as he did his 'children' in other epistles. If he came on too heavy, he could be rejected as interfering in their own affairs.

So he chose a 'cool' approach, reminding them of those aspects of the gospel which were relevant to the situation and likely to reduce the temperature and relieve the pressure. Once it is accepted that the basic need was reconciliation between resident Gentile believers and returning Jewish believers, the whole letter makes sense. In a subtle and inoffensive way, Paul 'bangs their heads together' all the way through.

He reminds the Gentiles of the appalling background of pagan perversion from which they have come, but rebukes the Jews for their moral superiority when they are guilty of the same things even while they condemn them. Jew and Gentile are alike; all have sinned, without the law of Moses or with it. Nobody is better than anyone else (3:9). Since our salvation depends on Christ's atonement and the imputing of its benefits to those who believe, acceptance with God (justification) is also exactly the same for Jew and Gentile (3:29f). Through faith, Jew and Gentile are alike sons of Abraham, the first to be so justified, before he was circumcised (Chapter 4). The real division is between the sons of Abraham, Jewish and

Gentile, and the sons of Adam (Chapter 5).

Paul then deals with the legacy Gentile believers bring from their past, namely, licence, an indulgence rationalised in terms of grace (Chapter 6); and the legacy Jewish believers bring from their past, that is, legalism, a bondage which leads to misery and despair (Chapter 7). Both need to enjoy a life of liberty in the Spirit, freeing them from sin and the law (Chapter 8).

Chapters 9–11, with this approach, form the climax towards which Paul has been building, rather than an inserted parenthesis. God has not rejected the Jewish people and their replacement is only temporary. There is no room for arrogance in Gentile believers (11:20); nor for Jewish arrogance, remembering that their people knowingly rejected their own Messiah (10:18f).

Even the ethical exhortations in chapters 12–15 are related to this basic theme. While paying some attention to the obvious question of relating to civic authorities in the metropolitan capital (the Gentile believers were reluctant to respect them and the Jewish believers to pay taxes), Paul's primary concern was with the internal matter of living together with believers of totally different backgrounds. Significantly, his teaching on 'coping with each other's scruples' (in Chapter 14) deals with food and special days, the very questions most likely to arise between Jewish and Gentile believers.

The reader is invited to reread the whole letter in the light of this analysis. They will find it an illuminating exercise, even if they are not convinced.

But why has this matter been raised at all in this book, albeit as an appendix? Its relevance to our discussion must now be demonstrated.

Many evangelicals, especially those deeply influenced by the Reformers, have taken the traditional line that Romans is a complete presentation of the gospel, containing all its essential elements. What is not here may be of value, but is not fundamental.

And, of course, the particular emphases of a charismatic viewpoint are almost unmentioned. Though there is a whole chapter (8) on life in the Spirit, there is no specific description of *how* the gift of the Spirit is received, though there is one mention of him being 'given' (5:5). There is only one mention of the exercise of spiritual gifts (12:6–8), though Paul expresses a desire to impart them (1:11) and another reference could, with some latitude, relate to tongues (8:26; but 'groans that words cannot express' are hardly languages!).

When 'Romans' is taken as a definition of the gospel, in isolation from other scriptures, the conclusion is drawn that the charismatic dimension is not important to our task of preaching the gospel and can even be a distraction from it ('Let's stop arguing about the baptism and gifts of the Spirit and get on with evangelism'). It is even possible to draw a theological as well as a practical inference from Romans, when treated in this way. Since Paul majored on justification by faith and made no separate point about receiving the Spirit, we may assume that for him they were one and the same thing; it is impossible to believe without receiving (8:9 is a favourite 'proof-text' for this, though that application depends on a particular interpretation of 'have' and 'his'; many translators have taken the liberty of adding a second 'Christ' to undergird their own interpretation). This is to ignore the fact that the book of Acts reveals that Paul clearly distinguished between 'believing' and 'receiving' (as we saw in Chapter 9 of this volume).

It is also to overlook John the baptiser's testimony to the ministry of the coming Messiah as the one who would take away the sin of the world and baptise in Holy Spirit (John 1:29, 33).

And for Peter the two great benefits of the gospel were the forgiveness of sins and the gift of the Spirit (Acts 2:38). Incidentally, forgiveness is not specifically mentioned once in Romans; what conclusion do we draw from that?

There is, in fact, a much simpler and more straightforward explanation for the omission of 'charismatic' distinctives in the letter to the Romans. That was not their problem! There was no reason to bring them up. Whereas the problems at Corinth demanded a totally different kind of letter. Paul's teaching there is just as important to the 'gospel' as his letter to the Romans. In neither case is he attempting to summarise Christian doctrine or define the gospel. In both cases, he is selecting those Christian doctrines most relevant to the situation in hand and addressing them to those who had already received the gospel and the Spirit, so did not need either spelled out to them again.

APPENDIX B

TONGUES AS 'A SIGN FOR UNBELIEVERS'

There is a widespread practice among charismatics called 'singing in the Spirit'. Congregations are encouraged to engage in a spontaneous harmonising in tongues. While the music is co-ordinated, usually by moving up and down a major chord, the words are not, since no 'interpretation' is given.

Is there scriptural warrant for this? Paul sang praise, sometimes 'with the mind' and sometimes 'with the spirit' (note the small 's'; he refers to his own spirit, not the Holy Spirit, though he believed the latter was providing the words). But he only did this in private, when he was alone with the Lord.

In public, he forbade the use of tongues without interpretation, since they were not 'edifying'. How, then, can the corporate use of tongues without interpretation be justified?

The question arises out of an apparent contradiction

between Acts 2 and 1 Corinthians 14 and another within the latter chapter. It has very practical implications for worship and evangelism.

Should 'tongues' be used in the presence of unbelievers without the gift of interpretation to render them intelligible? If so, how can that be of positive value to them? If not, why not?

Some take the day of Pentecost as a precedent. Certainly, over a hundred people were simultaneously praising the Lord in unlearned and newly given languages and this deeply impressed spectators, providing Peter with an audience to which he could preach the gospel. Before taking this as an encouragement to use tongues as a method of evangelism, or rather, pre-evangelism, some qualifications need to be added to our summary statement.

First, the tongues were originally given in a private or semi-private context, before the situation became public. The disciples were more probably in a corner of the temple, possibly Solomon's Porch where the Mosque Al-aqsa now stands, than the upper room; it was the time for morning prayer and the crowd came to them, not vice-versa.

Second, the content of their new languages was directed to God rather than man; it was praise rather than preaching.

Third, they did not decide to speak in tongues in order to evangelise. It was a spontaneous release after being filled with Holy Spirit. On no subsequent occasion did they try to repeat the effect on the bystanders. Nor is there any later example of this happening in a public context.

Fourth, not all the spectators were impressed with a sense of the supernatural. Some interpreted such abandoned behaviour as the result of intoxication.

Fifth, the tongues given on this occasion were carefully chosen by God (out of six thousand possible languages of men, to say nothing of those used by angels; 1 Cor 13:1) and they corresponded to those spoken by the crowd of pilgrims who had 'come home' to Jerusalem from the 'diaspora' (dispersion) to celebrate the feast. There is no scriptural guarantee that tongues given will always be recognisable.

That there have been, and still are, occasions when God arrests the attention of unbelievers by giving a word in a language they know but the speaker does not, I have no doubt. I have had personal experience of this (a lady in the Colston Hall, Bristol, spoke perfect Urdu in the presence of myself and a Pakistani, who recognised his home dialect) and have received not a few first-hand reports.

But after Pentecost there is no mention of this possible effect of tongues. The emphasis falls on edification inside the church rather than evangelism outside. The fact that the 'gift' of interpretation is listed alongside tongues suggests that in normal use the languages will not be recognised by anyone present and will require a supernatural ability to be translated.

It is in this context that Paul apparently discourages the *corporate* use of tongues in the presence of unbelievers, for the precise reason that they will not understand what is being said (or sung) and are even more likely to assume the worst ('out of their mind', which in a sense is true!).

However, in the middle of these strictures on the corporate exercise of tongues comes an astonishing assertion: 'Tongues, then, are a sign, not for believers but for unbelievers' (1 Cor 14:22). At first sight this directly contradicts its context, as if Paul is saying that tongues are intended for unbelievers, so don't give them a chance to hear them! Some commentators are convinced a scribal error has crept in to an early copy of Paul's letter, reversing his words and in effect making him say the exact opposite of what he actually intended (J.B. Phillips had no hesitation in reversing it back again in his translation, to what he believed was the original statement).

Others, wanting scriptural warrant for the corporate use of tongues, have ignored the context and its prohibition. They argue that if tongues are a sign for unbelievers, their presence should encourage us to use the gift, expecting it to attract and impress them, as at Pentecost.

It is one of those passages which has been used to support opposite and contradictory positions! Surely Paul must have intended one or the other, but hardly both. A more thorough exegesis is clearly needed. If 'a text out of context is a pre-text', we know where to begin.

The first letter to the Corinthians was sent to answer a number of questions and deal with a number of problems that had arisen in the fellowship there. Among these was the use (and abuse) of spiritual gifts, to which Paul devoted chapters 12–14 (we need to remember it is one section in the original, not three chapters). In Chapter 12 he deals with spiritual gifts; in Chapter 13 he deals with spiritual gifts, without love; in Chapter 14 he deals with spiritual gifts, with love. The last chapter is the 'more excellent way' (12:31; cf 14:1). He does not consider the possibility of love without gifts, at least not in this present age (13:8–13).

Using the gifts in love involves a self-restraint springing from a caring concern for others. In corporate worship, the edification of others takes precedence over self-expression. It is only possible to reach the spirits of others through their understanding, therefore all corporate acts of worship must be intelligible to all participants. A few individual tongues may be allowed, but only if an interpreter is known to be present and can translate them for the others. Prophecies do not present the same problem, but even they become unhelpful in unrestricted quantity.

It is entirely consistent with these maxims that Paul should discourage the corporate use of tongues in the presence of the 'uninitiated' (those who have not yet been introduced to them and therefore are unable to participate) and 'unbelievers'. But why does he not just say this? Why introduce this point of tongues being 'a sign for unbelievers'? And how can that possibly fit in with his restrictions?

It is hardly surprising that Paul calls for 'adult thinking' on what he is about to say (14:20)! His argument is not simple. But it is coherent.

The key is to ask: 'What are tongues a sign of for the unbeliever?' Any 'sign' points beyond itself to something else (as road signs point to hazards ahead). A sign is not significant in itself, but indicates the reality of a situation beyond itself. So what does the sign of tongues indicate to an unbeliever?

In quoting Isaiah 28:11f (which is paralleled in Isaiah 33:19 and Jeremiah 5:18), Paul gives us the clue. When God's people in Israel stopped trusting and therefore obeying him, his judgement took the form of bringing a foreign invader (the Babylonians) to occupy their land and even his city of Jerusalem. In their own streets they would be surrounded by 'strange tongues', which they would not understand. They would feel excluded, which in a real sense they were, for these 'tongues' would be a 'sign' of their rejection by God.

In the same way, an unbeliever, surrounded by languages he does not understand, will feel excluded, rejected, unwanted. He will feel that he doesn't belong there, that that is not the place for him. He will not feel 'at home' with what is going on and will want to leave.

A fellowship that wants him to feel included and involved will concentrate on prophecy rather than tongues. An intelligible message may well touch his heart and he will become more conscious of the divine presence, revealing his sinful secrets, yet in a way that will hold him, draw him closer, and he will find himself participating in the worship.

But that just raises another problem of equal perplexity. In the same context, Paul says that prophecy is 'for believers, not unbelievers'. The plot thickens! Actually, this phrase is even more difficult to make sense of than the other. We may note the omission of the word 'sign'; prophecy is significant in itself by being immediately intelligible and therefore directly meaningful.

Paul is drawing this conclusion about prophecy from the same Old Testament quotation. If speaking in strange tongues is a sign of rejection, speaking in a familiar tongue is a sign of acceptance. If the one is for those who don't want to believe in God, the other is for those who do. God speaks *plainly* to those who want to hear what he says (even Jesus spoke obscurely when people didn't want to understand; Matt 13:10–15; cf Isa 6:9f).

It is vital to realise that Paul is talking about unbelievers who have *come in* to a gathering of believers (14:23). To do so in those days was a bold step (Acts 5:13f). If anyone did, it could and should be assumed that they were wanting to become believers and wanted to hear from God. The words Paul puts in their mouths on hearing prophecy assume they already have the minimal faith required to seek God (14:25; cf Heb 11:6 – note the word 'comes'). An unbeliever who 'comes in' is to be regarded as a potential, if not an actual, believer. God wants him to feel he belongs, to sense he has come 'home'. Above all, God wants to talk to him, through the mouths of his people. He wants them to prophesy. He wants the 'seeker' to understand, because the seeker wants to understand. A 'sign' of rejection would be totally inappropriate.

APPENDIX C

CHARISMATIC GIFTS

A paper given at the National Assembly of Evangelicals in Church House, Westminster, in October, 1966, and later published in *Unity in Diversity* (Evangelical Alliance, 1967)

It was inevitable that this subject should come before this Conference; it was not inevitable that the lot should fall upon me – but it has done so! It was inevitable because of the old pentecostalism and because of the new pentecostalism. The old has come of age, indeed pensionable age; it is now just over 60 years old and is rapidly on its way to becoming the largest Protestant denomination in the world, not yet in England but on the world scale, the largest; furthermore it has recently had great publicity in the publication of *The*

Cross and the Switchblade and other kindred literature, which has aroused a tremendous amount of interest, particularly among the lay members of our churches. Coupled with the old pentecostalism, which is now old enough to join the Free Church Federal Council, the World Council of Churches, and other things, and is rapidly becoming 'respectable', is the new pentecostalism, which has invaded the historic denominations, not from the top but from the bottom. Now because of these two facts it was inevitable that this subject should be brought up either this year or next year. Perhaps even the peak of the crisis over this is already past but it is still a matter at issue for us to look at charitably, scripturally and lovingly together.

May I make a personal testimony? My interest in charismatic gifts is not due to contact with either the old or new pentecostalism, though I have had some very happy fellowship with both. It was originally due to a brief and careful study of the Scriptures and what they had to say about the Holy Spirit. An impartial study of the Scriptures – and no other book on this subject – raises some very serious questions, and I want to bring six questions before you which I have had to face and answer to the best of my ability for myself, which you must face and come to your own convictions. If you differ from me, let us agree to differ without being disagreeable!

The first question is, 'Since it is obvious that charismatic gifts were part of the early church's life, can we have them today?' I have met a few people who have tried to say that because the charismatic gifts are only mentioned in the Epistle to the Corinthians, that therefore they were comparatively limited even in the early church. The same argument would also suggest that the Lord's Supper was equally limited, but that argument is never brought forward. It is quite clear that charismatic gifts were a normal and vital part of early church life, and any Christianity that seeks to base itself on the pattern of the New Testament church will have to ask the question, 'Can we have these today?'

Three answers are being given with a very emphatic negative. First, the Dispensationalist attitude, which would divide even Christian church history into periods with separate characteristics for each, and would suggest that charismatic gifts belong to the Apostolic age alone. That is the first negative answer. I think history is against them, but that would not be a decisive factor; Scripture must decide it.

The second emphatic 'No' is what I would call the 'Revivalist' answer: that such supernatural events occur only in periods of revival, and are, therefore, as spasmodic as the period of miracles in the Old Testament, centred around Moses, Elijah and Elisha.

The third emphatic negative is what I would call the Calvinistic answer, which says this matter is entirely within the inscrutable will of God. If he decides to give these gifts, we will accept them; if he does not, we will neither expect nor ask for them. A great deal is made there of the text that he will 'divide these gifts severally as he will'. It is perfectly right that the gifts are in his will, but Paul is not there dealing with *whether* he will give them, but *what he will give* to each individual. It is not so much the withholding as the distribution of the gifts that lies within his will in 1 Cor. 12.

My own thinking had to come to grips with the latter part of Chapter 13 of 1 Corinthians, where it is clearly stated that these things will cease and pass away. The exegetical question is *when*? And the answer from the passage, in simple terms, is 'When the *perfect* is come' – when we see him face to face, and understand even as we have been fully understood. So, if you feel the perfect has come and you understand as fully as you have been understood, you can switch right off, now! But if, on the other hand, the question is open, and you feel – as a number of evangelical scholars do feel – that it is impossible to prove from Scripture that these gifts have passed away, or ought to have done, then you have to go on to a further question, 'Do we *want* them?'

I meet a lot of people who, frankly, would say, 'They're more bother than they're worth', and, 'We have managed quite well without them up to now; I don't really want such things.' As one dear lady said to me, 'I hope nothing supernatural is going to happen in our church.' Now considering the implications of Christian worship, this is a priceless remark, but I think I understand it.

There are three main reasons why people do not want charismatic gifts even if we can have them. The first is that they can be distracting. They can turn a person's mind away from holiness, evangelism, worship, and other things. Now there is an element of truth in that, and Paul talks about putting away childish attitudes in 1 Cor. 13, and some people have been like a child with a new toy. The phrase 'putting away childish things' does in fact refer to the Roman ceremony of Coming of Age, where a boy took his toys and took them to the temple and left them at the altar, and put away childish things . . . put away childish *attitudes* to things, too. Now, this is behind Paul's thinking; these can be distracting from other things if a person becomes absorbed in one part of the Christian faith and life. It is only part and there is an element of truth here.

Others feel that they are too disturbing; I mean by that that they are unexpected. When charismatic gifts are exercised it is not possible to write down on your Order Sheet exactly what is going to happen in the service, and it is very much more comfortable to know exactly what is going to happen; you have decided what will happen. The service will finish at the time you have decided. It is disturbing when the Holy Spirit takes over the order of worship and there are some who would rather not have that.

However, the greatest reason is this – that some have found them too dividing, and there is an element of truth in this. Churches have been split in recent days in this country over this very question. May I say very sincerely that I think this is as much due to bigotry on the one side as fanaticism on the other. There can be a mutual breakdown of relationships and it is not always the fault of those who have claimed to come into extra blessing – though it often has been. So there are those who would say 'It's not worth the game'; they are dividing, they are distracting, they are disturbing.

What does Scripture say? I cannot escape the conclusion that these charismatic gifts in the New Testament were not just limited to conserving the word of the apostles but were given to edify and build up the church as part of the church's equipment; only part of it, but a definite part of it.

I want to read you just three sentences from a book: 'It is not only through the Sacraments and church ministry that the same Holy Spirit sanctifies and leads the people of God and enriches it with virtues; allotting his gifts to everyone according to his will (1 Cor. 12:11), he distributes special graces among the faithful of every rank. By these gifts he makes them fit and ready to undertake the various tasks or offices advantageous for the renewal and upbuilding of the church. According to the words of the Apostle, "the manifestation of the Spirit is given to everyone for profit" (1 Cor. 12:7). These charismatic gifts, whether they be the most outstanding or the most simple and widely diffused, are to be received with thanksgiving and consolation, for they are exceedingly suitable and useful for the needs of the church.'

I have been naughty, I have been reading from *De Ecclesia*, the Roman Catholic Dogmatic Schema on the Church, of the Vatican Council. I think it would be a tragedy if we fire broadsides at them from this Assembly, and yet take these Scriptures less seriously than they do for our time. I believe their words are right at this point, for they are quoting Scripture at this point. These are given for building up the church; only part of our equipment, but a definite part of it, in the Lord's will.

Then the next question is, 'Shall we need them? We have surely got along very well without them for many years in many churches.' I think only someone who is complacent about our present situation could answer that one in the negative. 'Shall we need them?' There are three areas of church activity where the gifts would be a help. I am not among those who think we have found the answer: 'This is going to bring in the Kingdom tomorrow.' I would think of suggesting that there is profit in the exercising of charismatic gifts in three areas of church life. First, *Ministry*. One of the curses of the evangelical world at the moment is that we have our own versions of 'I am of Cephas . . . I am of Apollos.' Let me say that I don't see any way out of this as long as we rely on men with *natural* gifts dedicated to the Lord. Only as *supernatural* gifts are expected can we expect the Holy Spirit to be no respecter of persons in the matter of ministry.

You know how the Americans look for a minister, don't you? They look for a man with four gifts: preaching, pastoral, youth work and administrative ability. If you find a man with one, then you'll stay as you are at the moment; find a man with two, your church will grow; find a man with three, you'll become the main church in town; find a man with four – don't touch him, he's a freak!

Now church after church is looking for a man with all the gifts, and just hoping that their next man will have them. This is utter folly – God has not given all the gifts to one man. The glory of supernatural gifts is that they are not given in relation to natural gifts. A man may have many natural and few supernatural, or many supernatural and no natural gifts. This opens up the possibility of ministry of the laity.

Secondly, *Worship*. I have read book after book after book on Worship recently and they are all discussing the form of worship and not the content. It is not so much the form, but the content that matters according to my reading of the Scripture, or we would have been given an order of service in the New Testament. The real question is whether we are worshipping in the Spirit, not whether we use prayers out of a book. Rutualism is as dangerous as ritualism.

Now at this point may I have a little 'one into the slips' for the Brethren? You'll forgive me for saying this! I believe that in *form* you may well be nearer to the New Testament patterns of worship than many of us who use more set forms. But, frankly, unless there is room in your spontaneous worship for the charismatic gifts, that made it real and live in the New Testament days, you can get into as dead a state as we. Charismatic gifts are no respecters of sex either, and when a woman prophesies, she may have to wear a hat, but she is prophesying and ministering to the church! Worship is an area of life in the church in which the Holy Spirit's activity is needed more than at present in many of our churches and services.

The third area is *Evangelism*. Someone made this jibe to me: they talked about the evangelical bourgeoisie and the pentecostal proletariat. But there is enough truth in that jibe for us to pause. Sixty-five per cent of the British population are in the lower income bracket; that's modern language for 'working class'. And it's noticeable where these successful evangelical churches are on the map of Britain – and I speak as right on that map – mostly in a ring around London and the South Coast. We have to consider this fact, too, that in the industrial areas many of those who emphasise charismatic gifts are making headway, though some others are too. That's generalisation and there are exceptions and qualifications. I think evangelism is an area in which charismatic gifts, and an expectancy of the Holy Spirit to work through ordinary people who have not got great natural gifts, but who have the dynamic of the Holy Spirit within, can play a big part.

The next question, then, comes out of this: 'Would we recognise them if they came?' This will depend on two things; first, definition. As long as we can define prophecy in terms of expository preaching, and as long as we can define the gift of wisdom in terms of a well-read man, or the gift of knowledge in long experience likewise; as long as we think of spiritual songs to be found within the Billy Graham chorus book; then, frankly, we shall not recognise charismatic gifts when they come. One of the books which helped me profoundly to know what I was looking for is a book written by the late Donald Gee, whose death is a loss not only to the pentecostal movement, but to the evangelical world at large. Whether you agree with him or not these gifts are for today, his little book concerning spiritual gifts, to my mind, defines the gifts properly, which is the first step.

The second step in recognising such gifts is the matter of discernment. There are other spirits abroad, there are demonic counterfeits and imitations, sometimes on a large scale, and it is vital that the wheat be sorted from the chaff. You can either accept it all and be led straight into wrong channels, or deny it all and miss something that God may have for you. Discernment, not of men, but of spirits, is needed. It is one of the necessary gifts. I am as disturbed as anyone by what I have seen in both old and new pentecostalism which seems to me counterfeit and imitation. Things can be worked up, not sent down, and it is vital to distinguish.

But having said that, is it not logical to claim that the devil does not bother to counterfeit unless there is something real? Will Antichrist appear until Christ is about to appear? Of course there is imitation. The devil knows what he is doing. The worst case of this I have heard is of a travelling evangelist laying hands upon people's heads and telling them to say 'banana' backwards, telling them that they then had the gift of tongues and had been baptised in the Spirit. With that sort of thing I will have nothing to do; neither will any self-respecting pentecostal, never mind evangelical. But given all that, given all the evidence that Dr Kurt Koch has unveiled, nevertheless I personally have seen enough of the real thing to believe that

God has given such things to build up the church in love and to strengthen the ministry of the members, and I am afraid I will take a lot of convincing to leave that position. Would we recognise them? Discernment and definition are vital.

The next question is, could we handle them? Frankly, most of our church organisations couldn't. It's like new wine in an old bottle. The primitive church couldn't handle it properly; and many churches today have not been able to handle this. But the alternative to abuse is not disuse, but proper use.

I want now to say something about what I have found to be the biggest stumbling block of all to those who were not sympathetic to this subject. 'How can those gifts be real in an absence of orthodoxy, holiness, and unity?' I want to say this: these gifts can be exercised by carnal Christians, who are not orthodox, not holy, and not united. Otherwise you would have to write off the Corinthian church. They were heterodox on the matter of the resurrection; their holiness left a great deal to be desired, and they got drunk at the Lord's table, which doesn't happen in your church. Those who would dismiss spiritual gifts because of the character of those who exercise them are not applying the scriptural tests. To those who do exercise them, I would say this. The gifts do not automatically bring holiness, orthodoxy, or unity, and these need to be sought as well, if the gifts are to be handled rightly. It is just as wrong to dismiss the gifts because these things are absent as to think that they are present because the gifts are. The whole thing hangs together or – to put it another way – without the fruit of the Spirit, the gifts are useless. If I had to choose I would rather be in a church that had the fruit and not the gifts than a church that had the gifts and not the fruit.

But is that the biblical alternative? Is Paul saying to us, 'Do you want them?' No, he does not say that, he says that the only coveting a Christian is allowed is to covet spiritual gifts. You are not only allowed to covet, you are exhorted to covet, spiritual gifts that other people exercise. Paul would say the gifts and the fruit are partners. Chapter 12 of 1 Cor. describes the gifts, Chapter 13 describes the fruit, and the climax is reached in Chapter 14, which tells you how to put them together in the local church or assembly. The climax is not Chapter 13. If we lick the jam out of the sandwich, and leave the two chapters on either side, we shall miss the point.

Now let me come finally to the most serious question of all for this Conference. I know that within this assembly we have different viewpoints and different convictions. I am very much in No-man's land; I am shut out from both sides for being too pentecostal and not pentecostal enough. I have had from sad personal experience knowledge of the fact that certain avenues of ministry are closing to anyone sympathetic to charismatic gifts, from the highest Conventions in the land downwards, and speaking engagements have been cancelled. This eases my diary but not my heart.

Must we divide over this? That is my final question. If we are agreed on the person and the work of the Father, and on the person and work of the Son, and on the person of the Holy Spirit and part of his work, and only differ on *part* of his work, is there a scriptural reason for not wanting fellowship with each other or dividing over this? I think not, and I think we must be very careful that this should not divide. It does mean that theological issues are raised. Is being 'born of the Spirit' the same as being 'baptised in the Spirit' or are these two different things? Is receiving the person of the Spirit the same as receiving the power of the Spirit? Or are these two different things? I know it raises questions like this. But are these questions to be thrashed out in separate groups, suspicious of one another, or are they to be thrashed out together in fellowship? I want to read a sentence from a book written about a controversy that split evangelicals formerly, but which is dying down now, namely eschatological truth. And I lift from the preface of this book a sentence which sums up my sentiments here: 'Suppose you are not convinced, shall we who are relying on the same Redeemer, begotten by the same God, inhabited by the same Spirit, incorporated in the same body, entrusted with the same Gospel, assaulted by the same devil, hated by the same world, delivered from the same hell, and destined for the same glory, shall we who have so much in common allow ourselves to be divided in heart or service because – just because – we are of different minds on this matter? God forbid.'